CASTLE COLORING BOOK

THIS BOOK BELONGS TO:

____

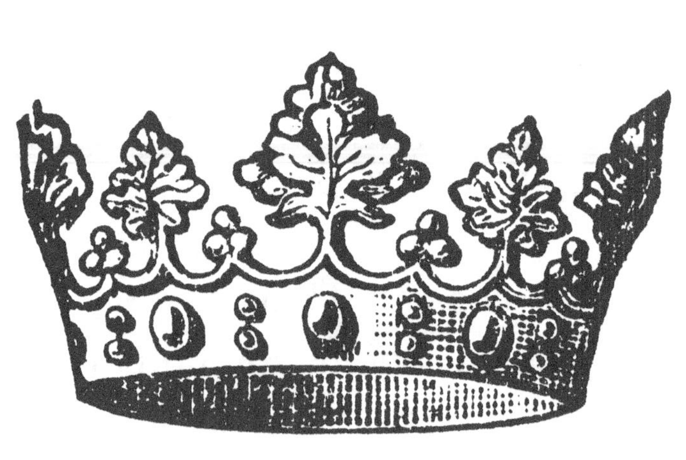

P. V. Alverson

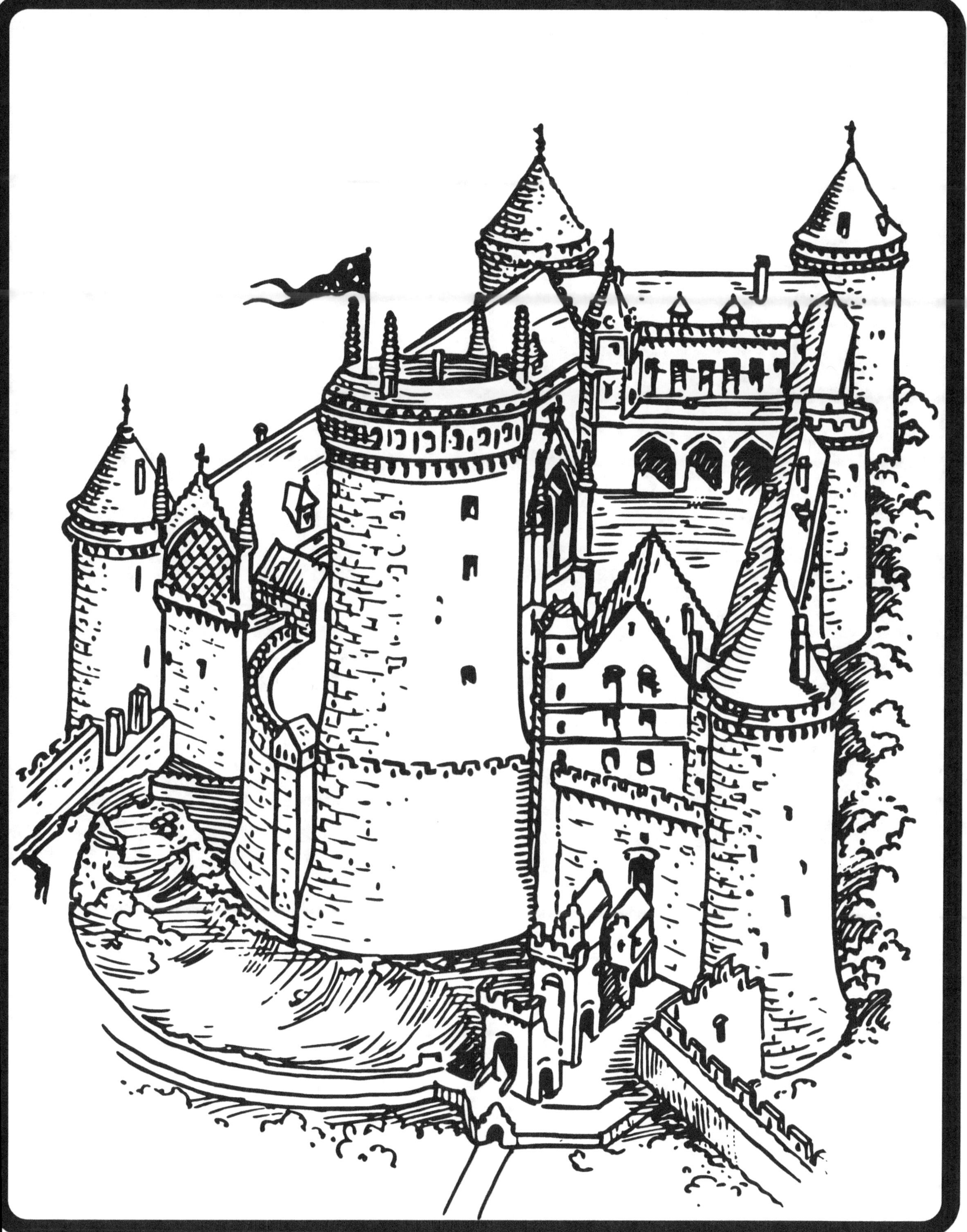

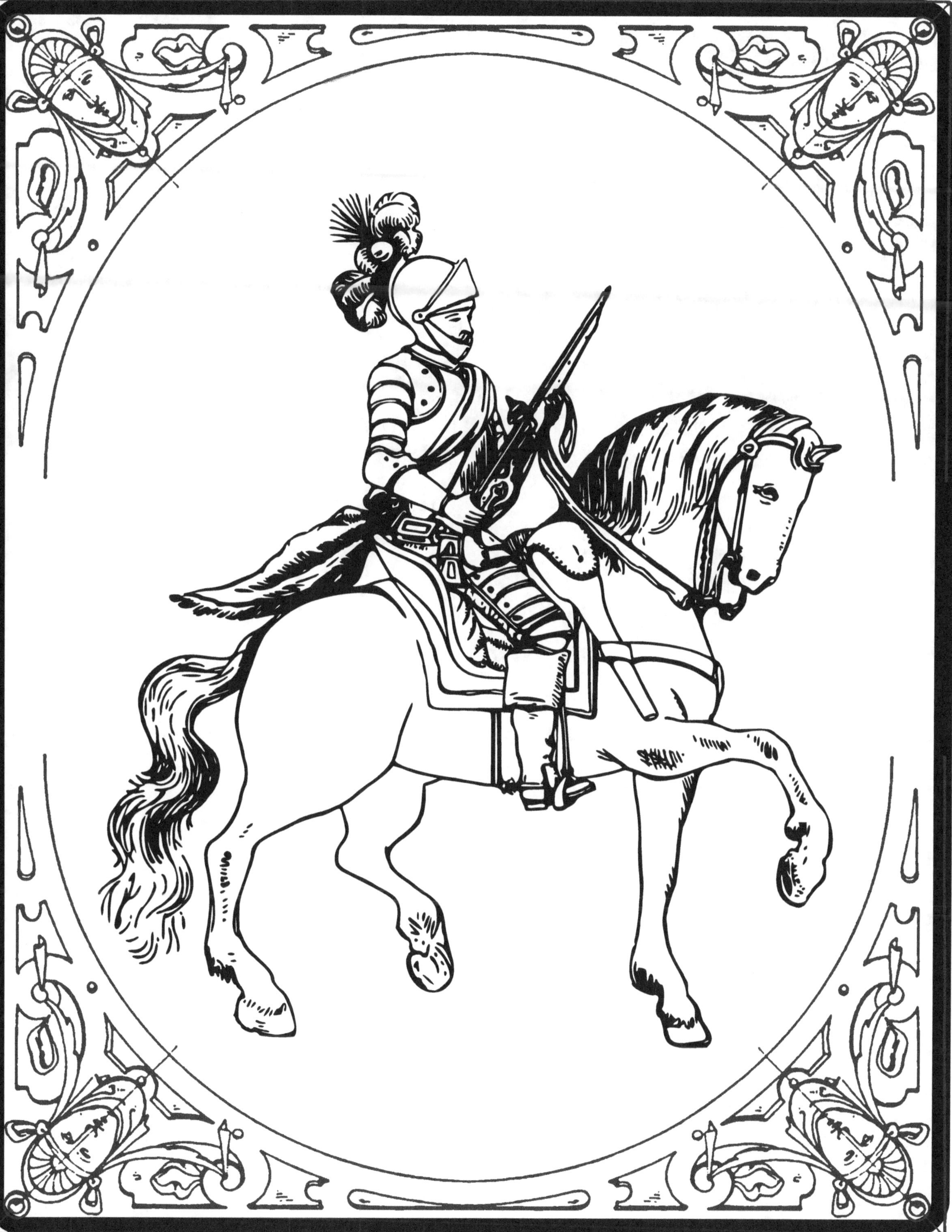

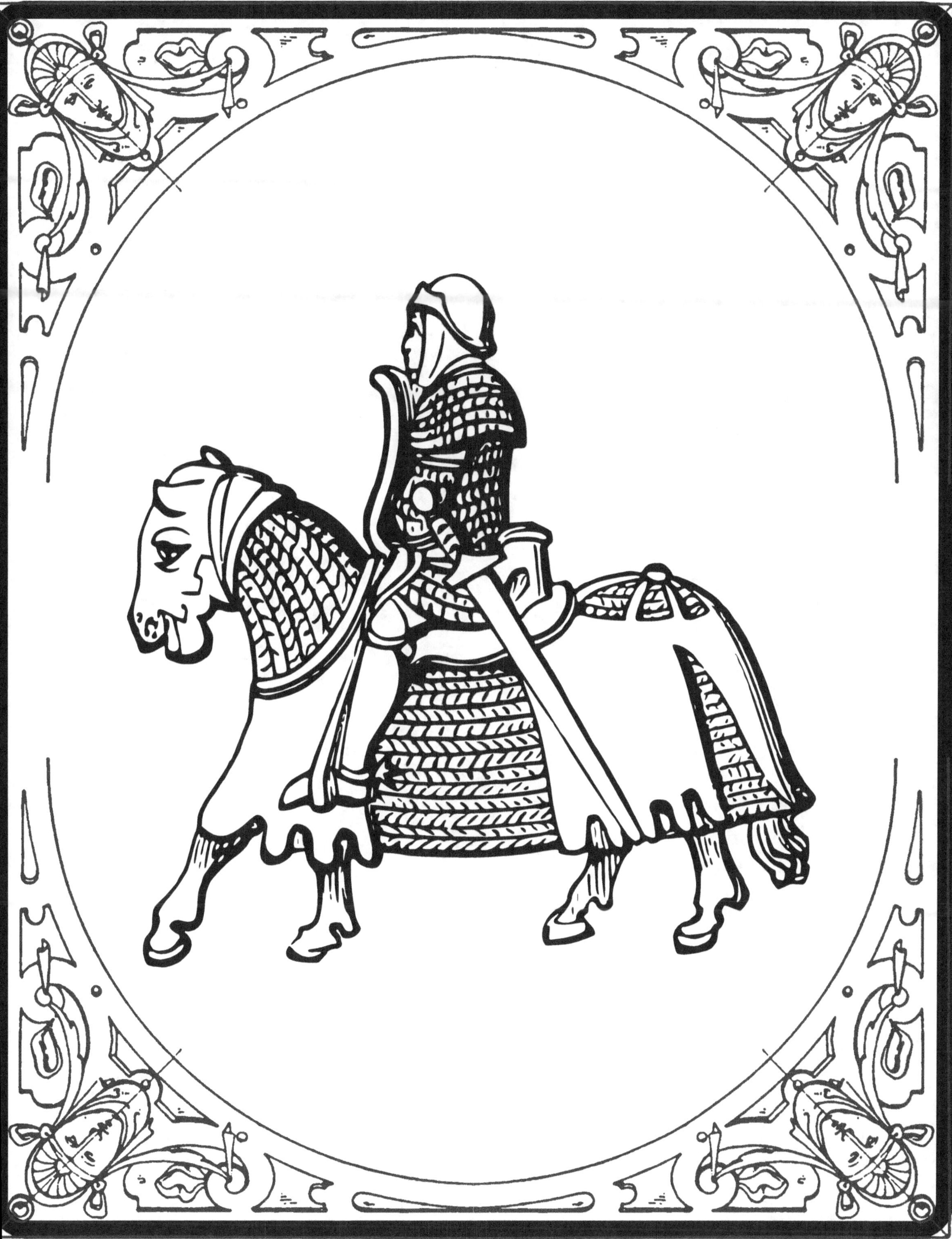

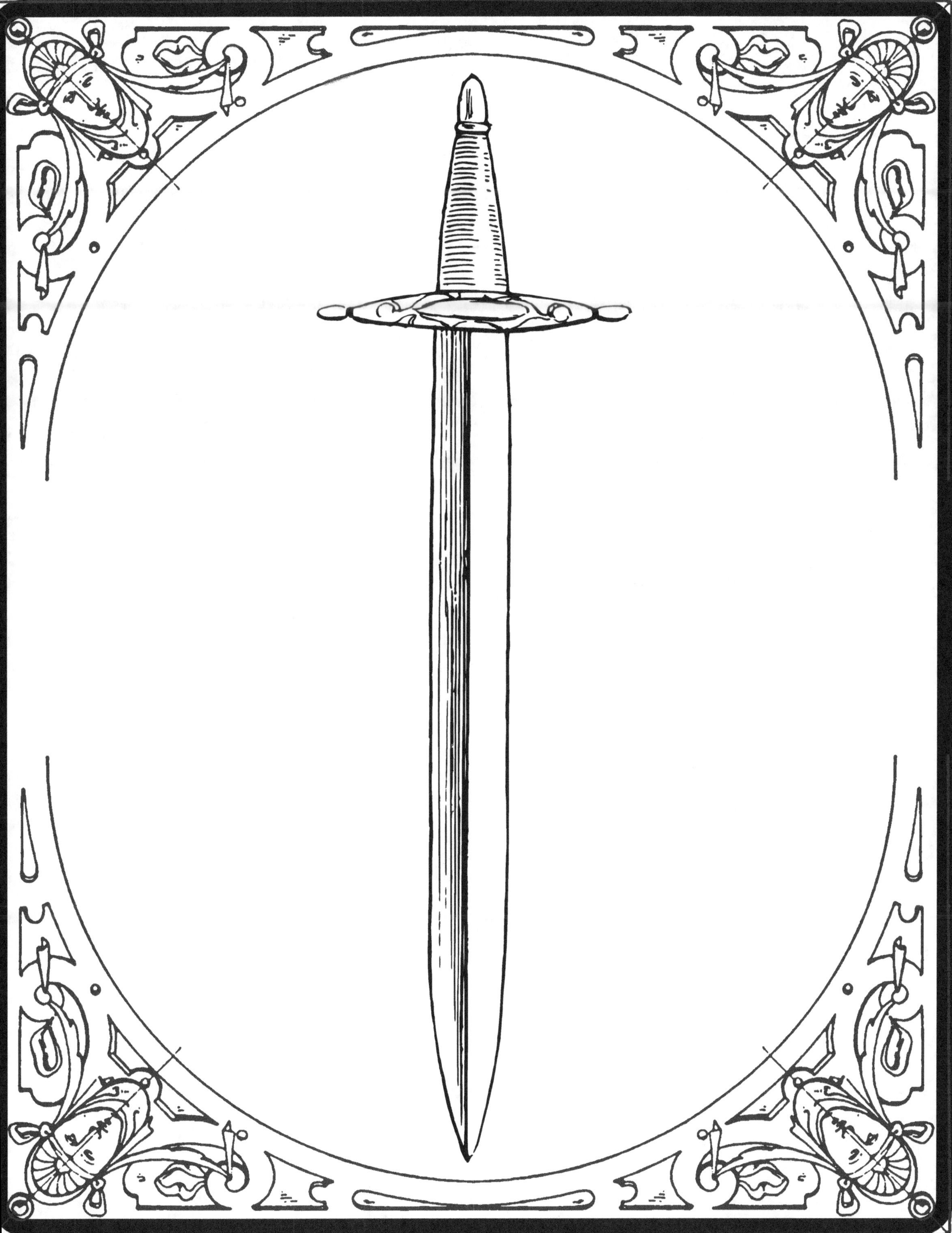

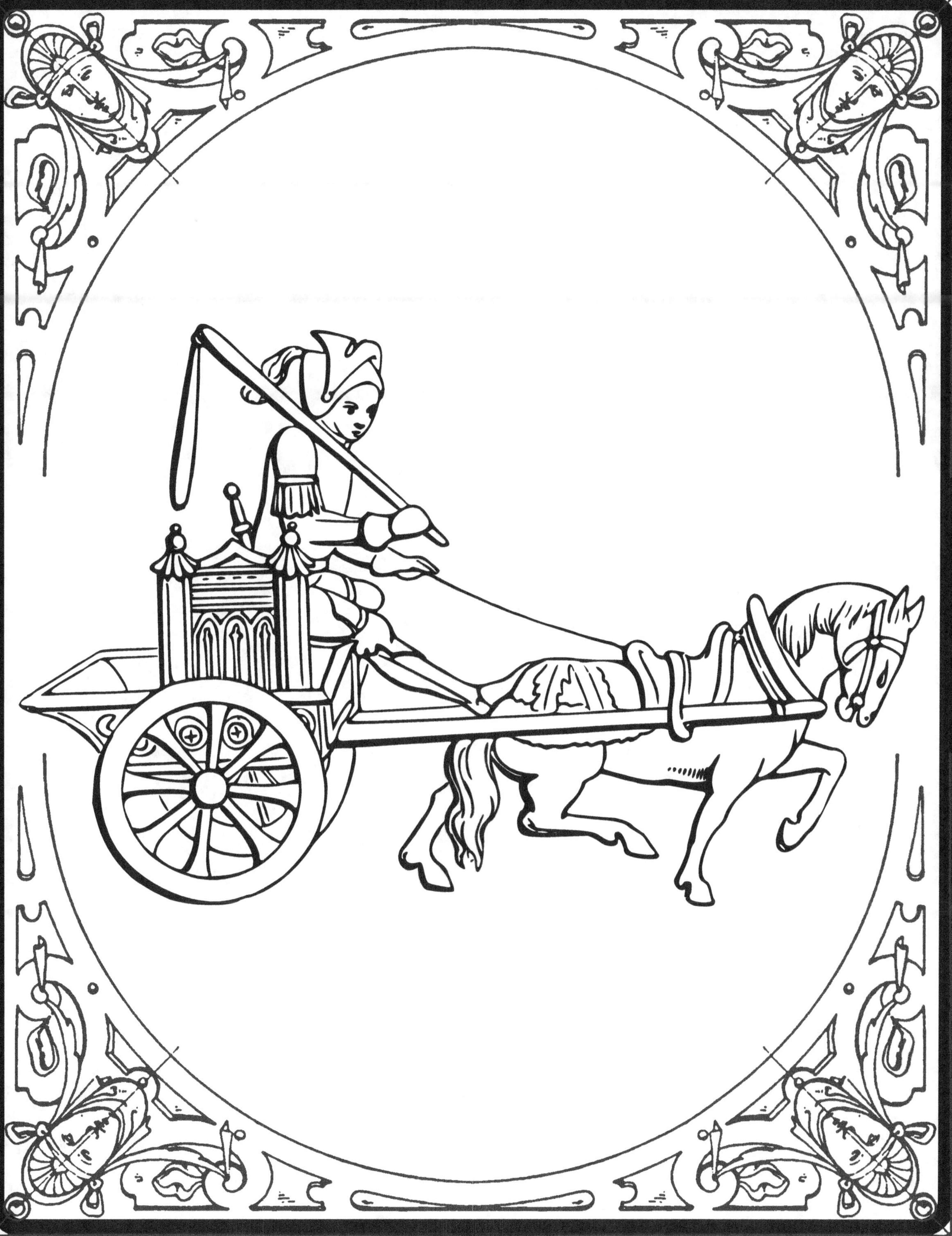

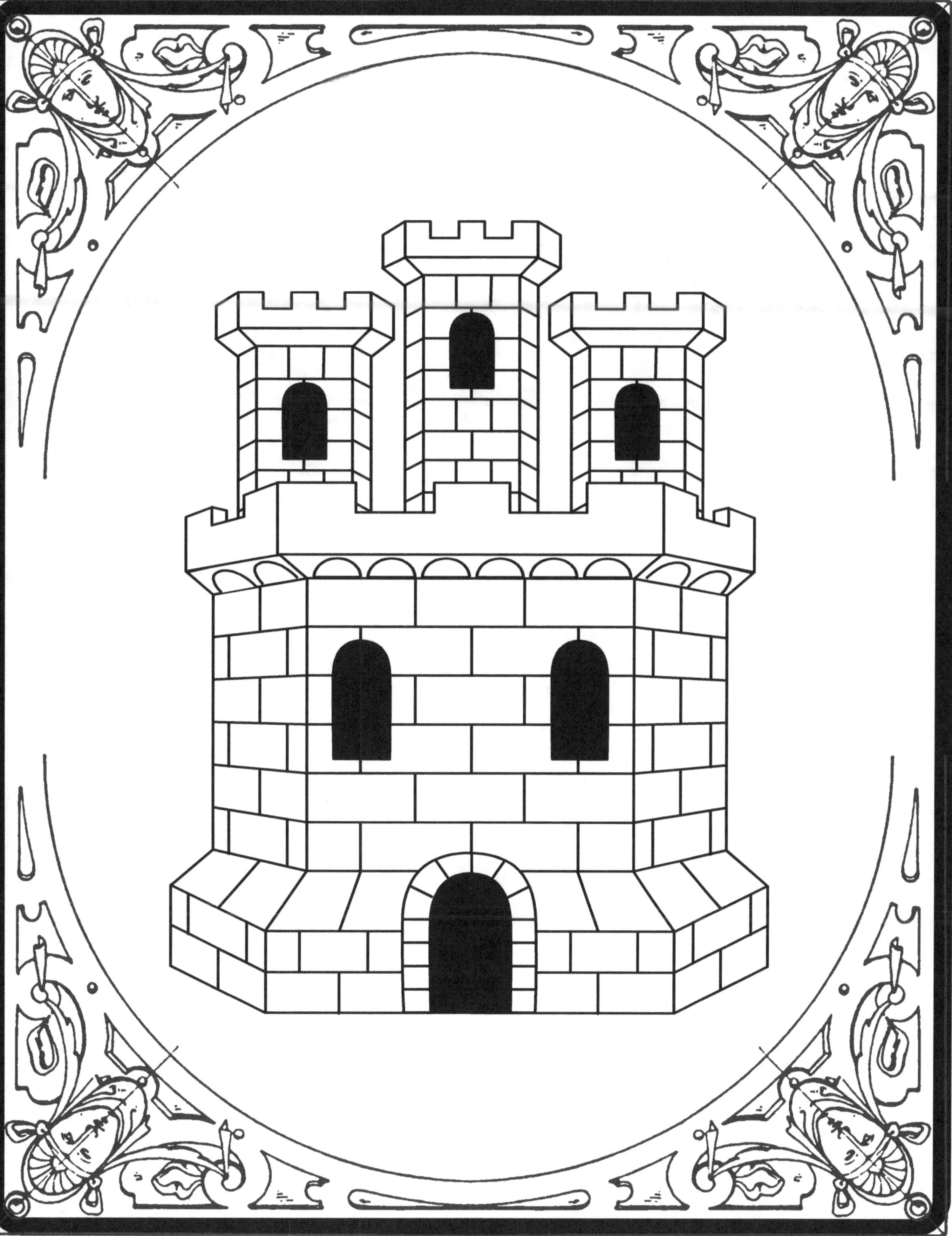

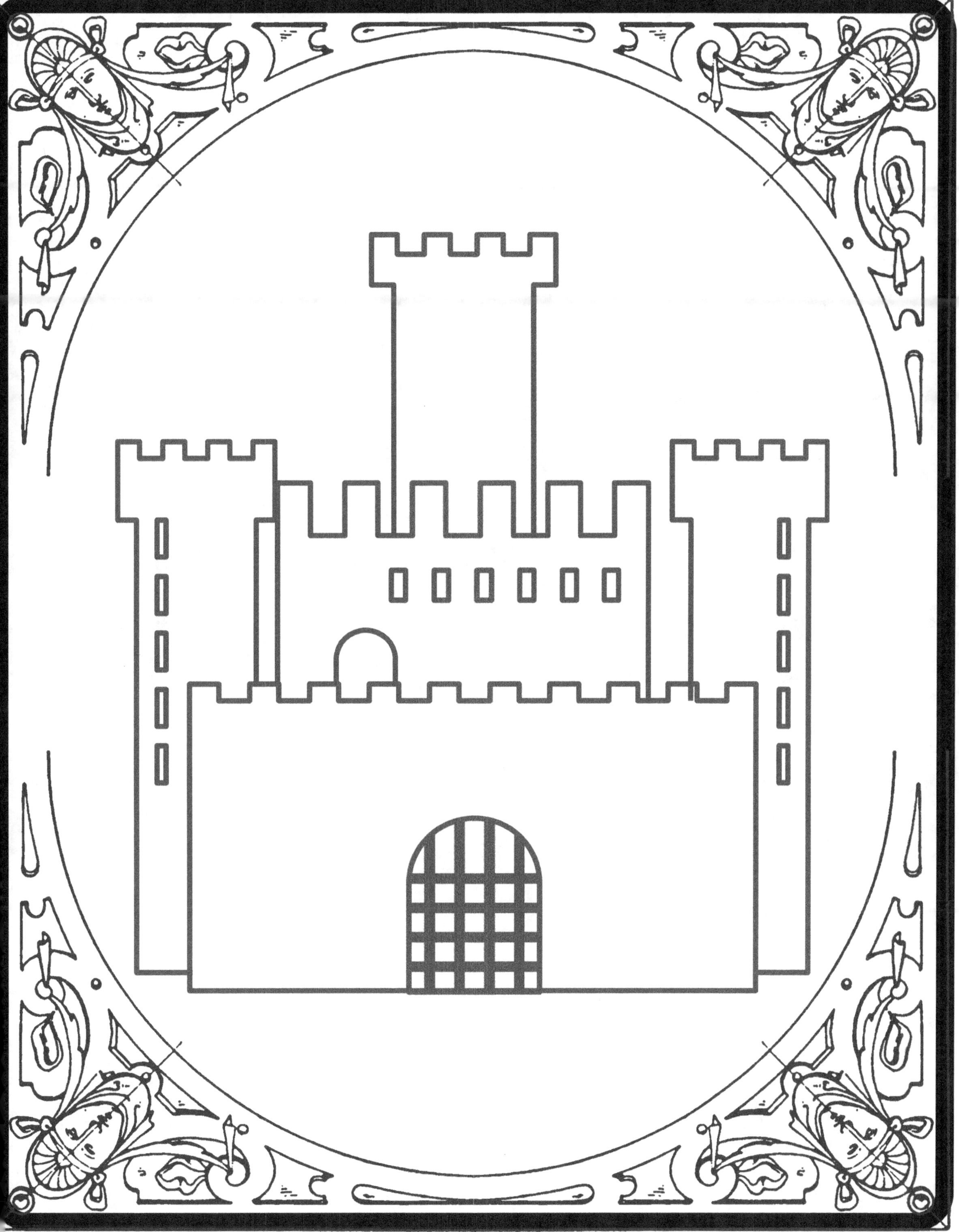

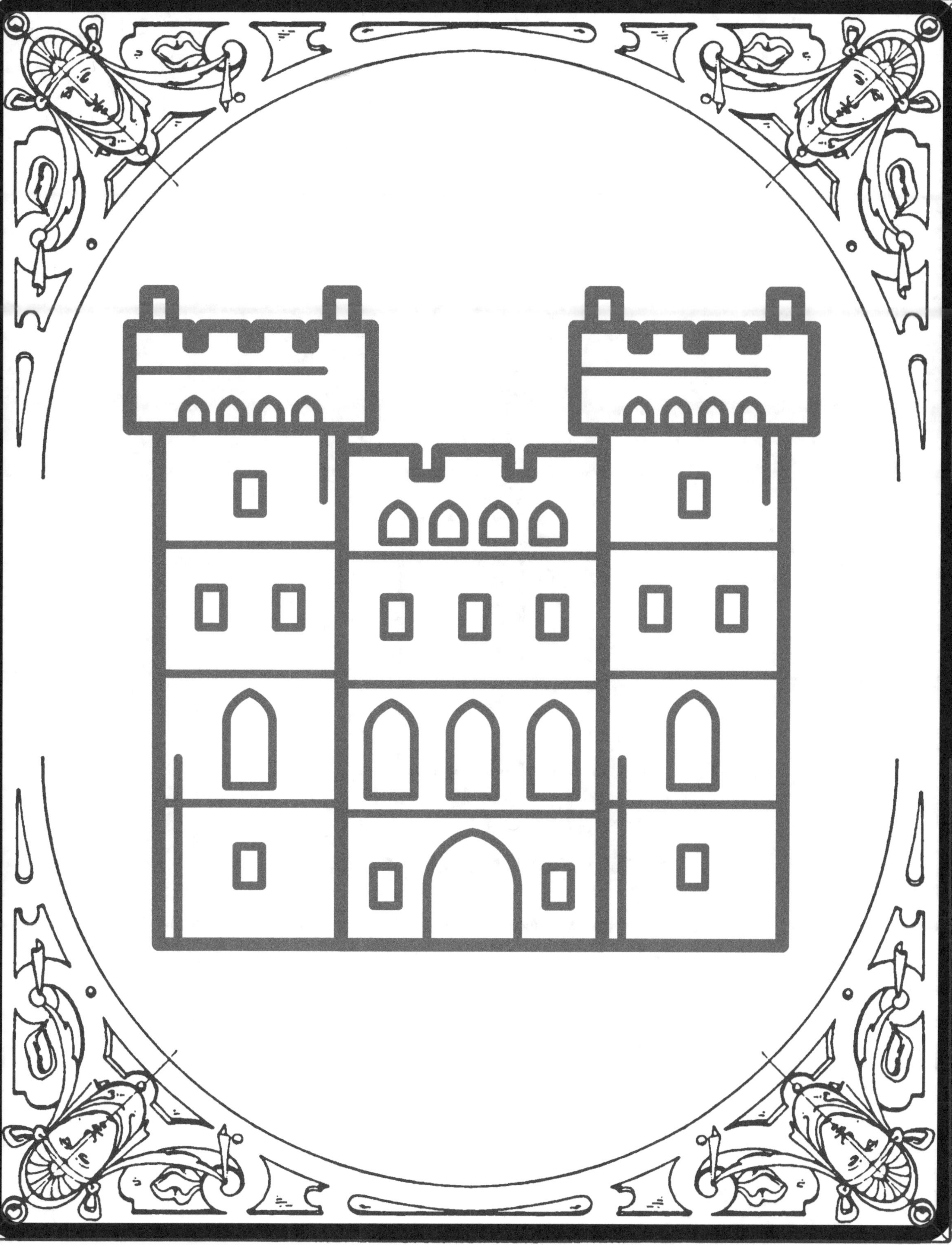

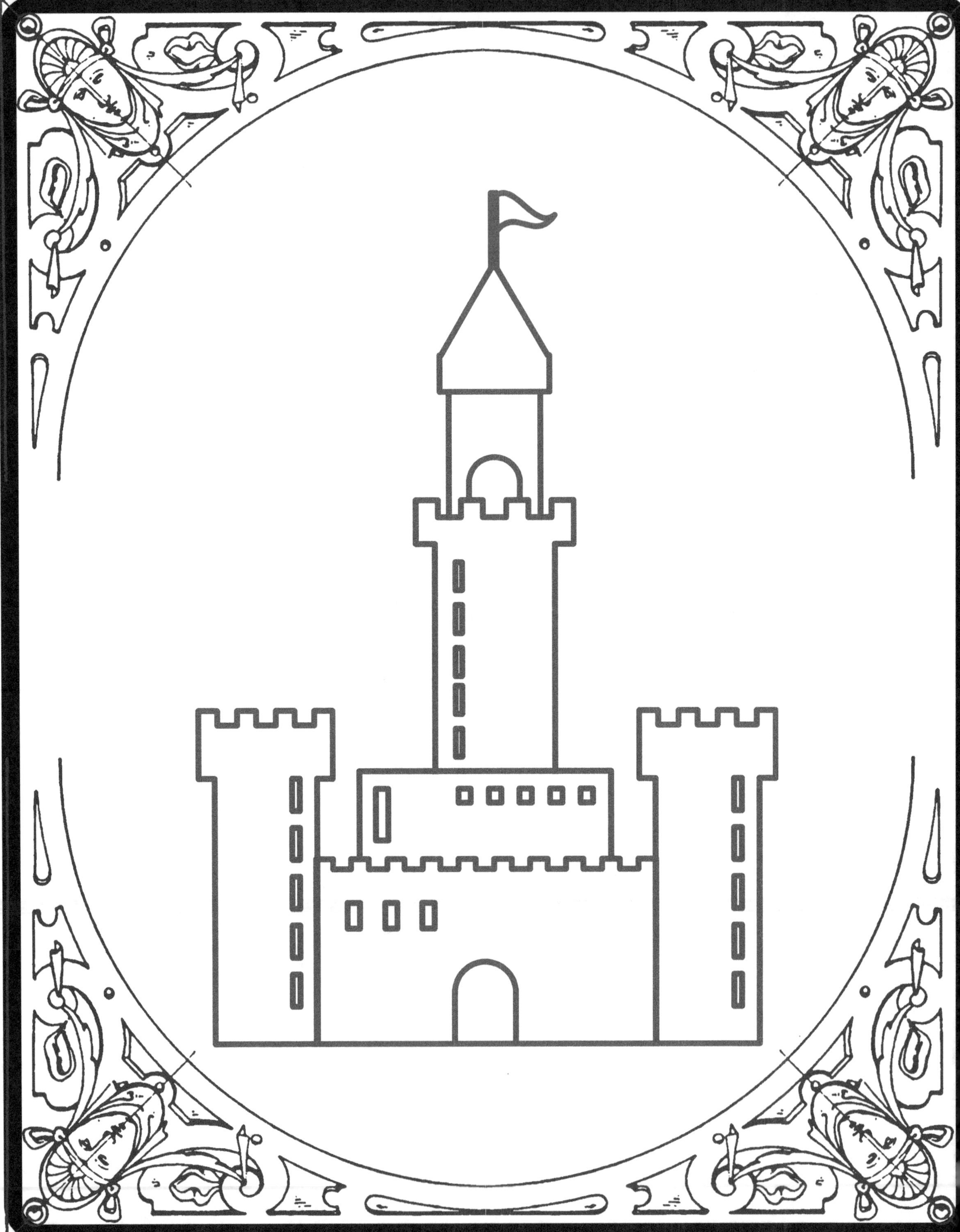

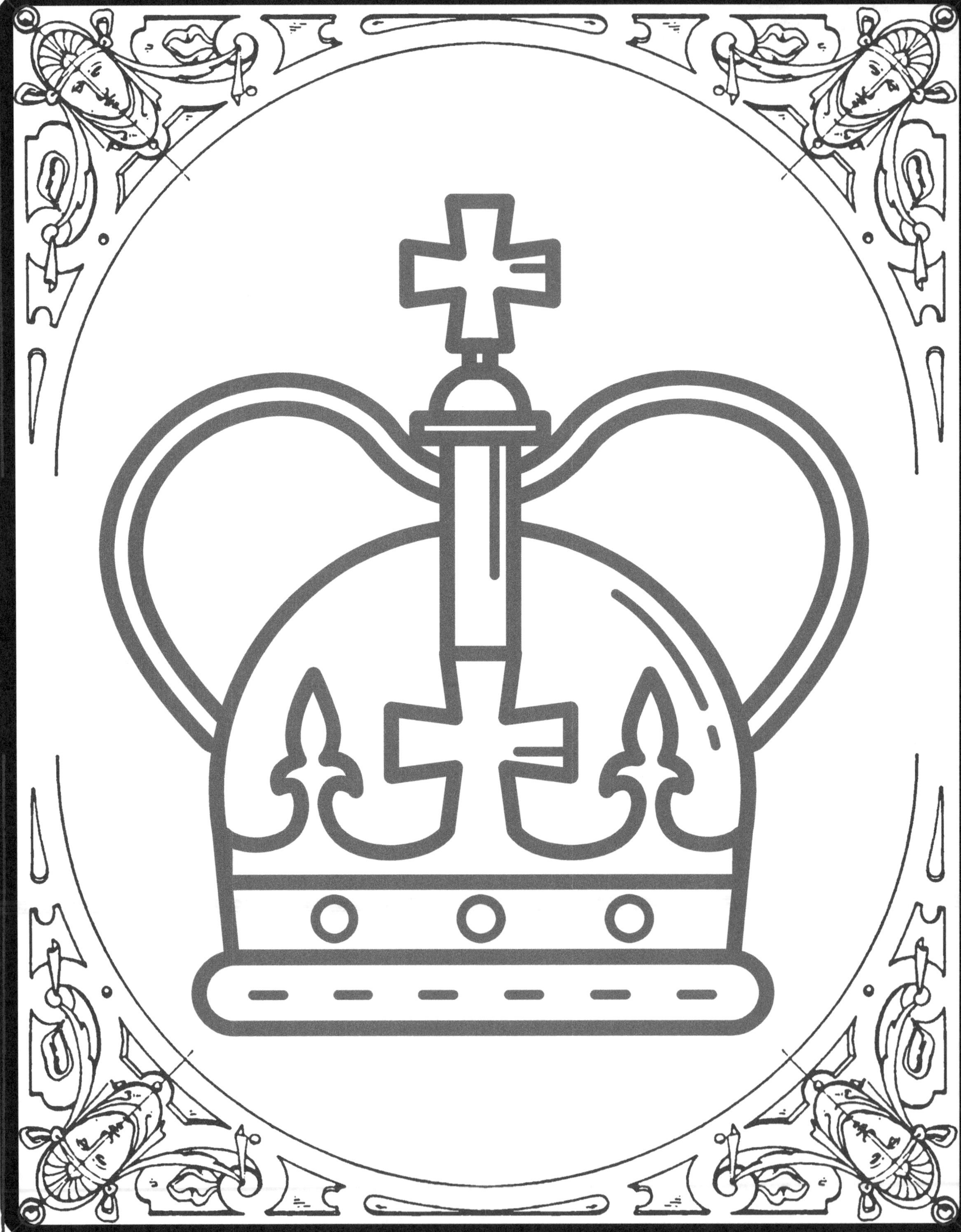

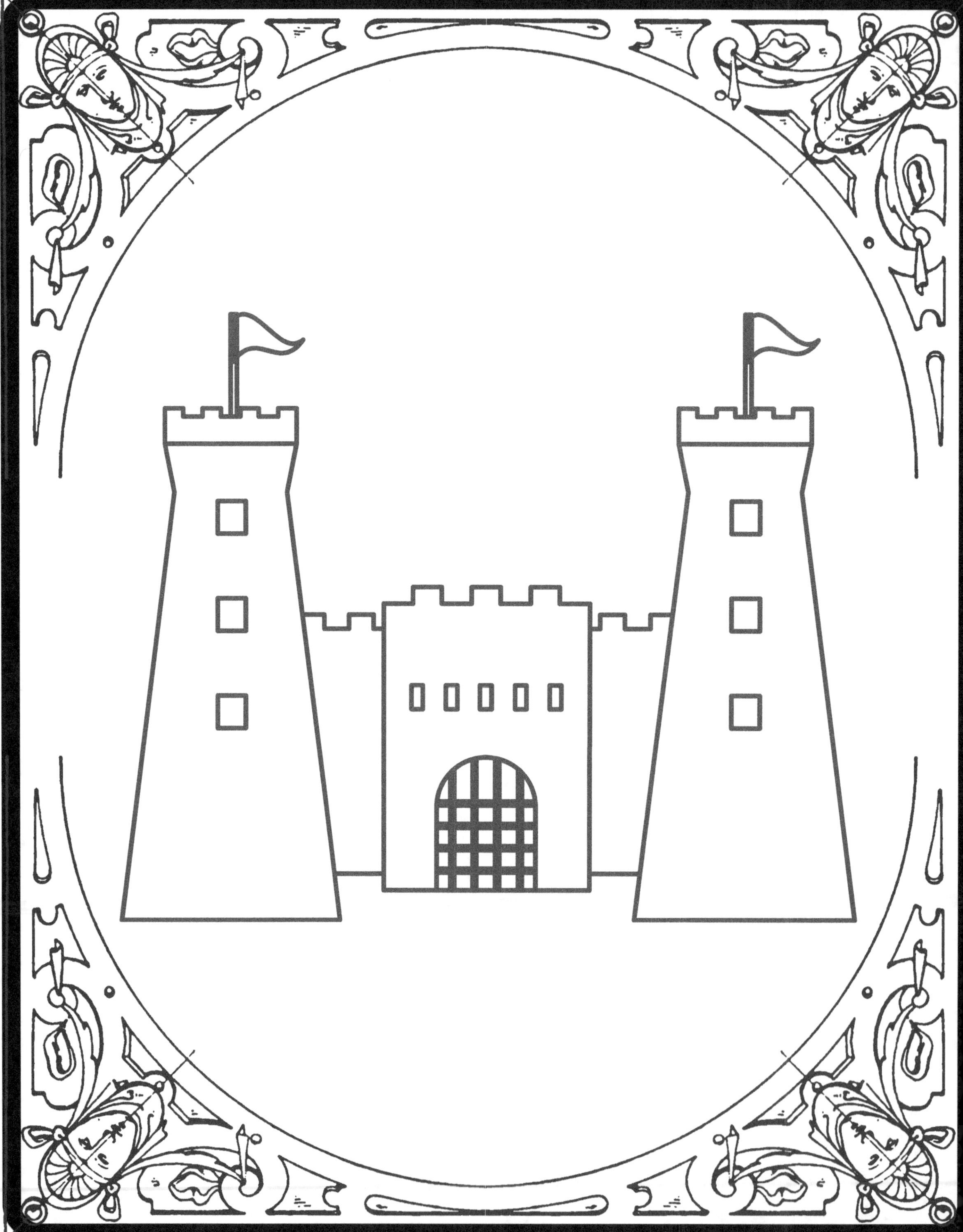

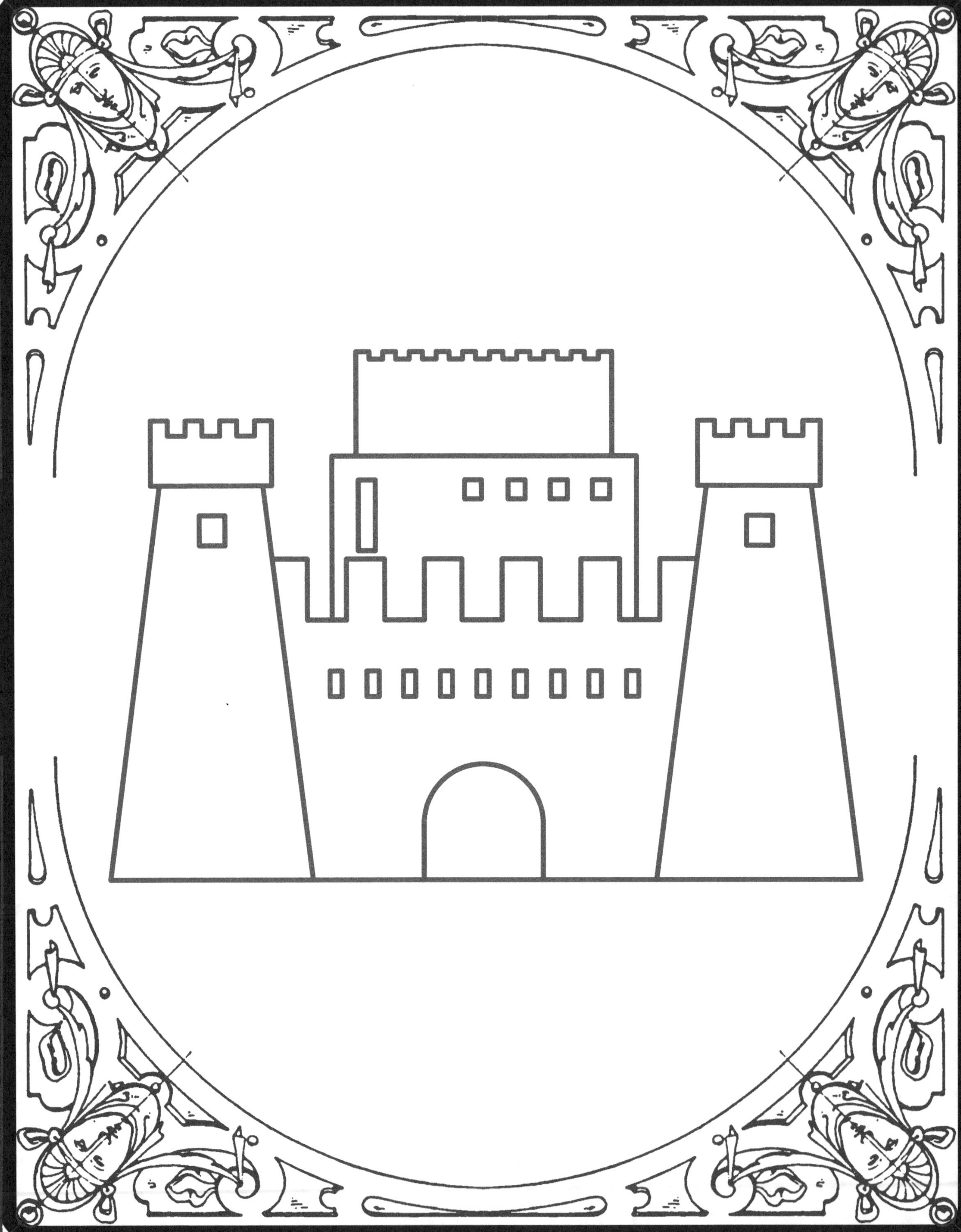

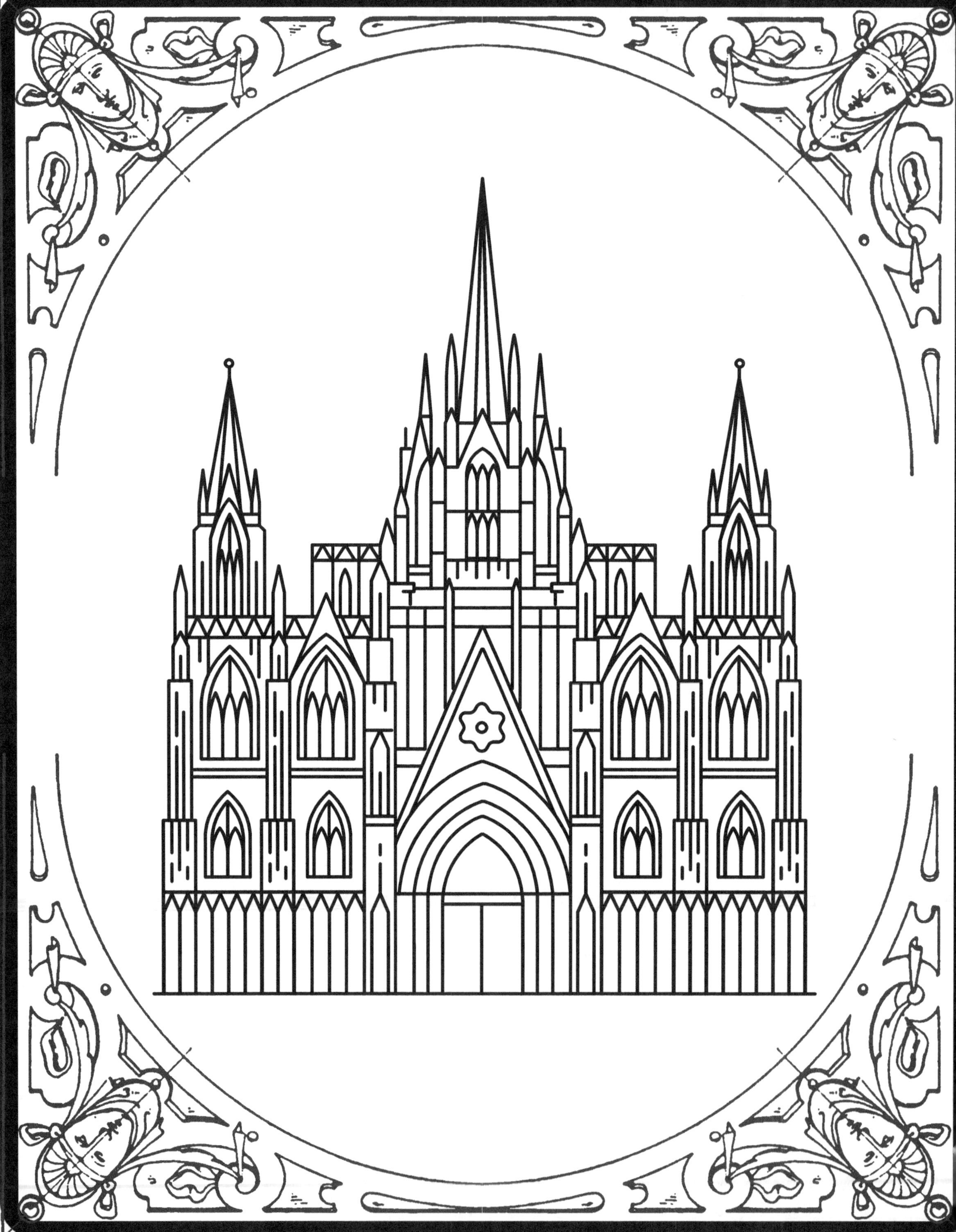

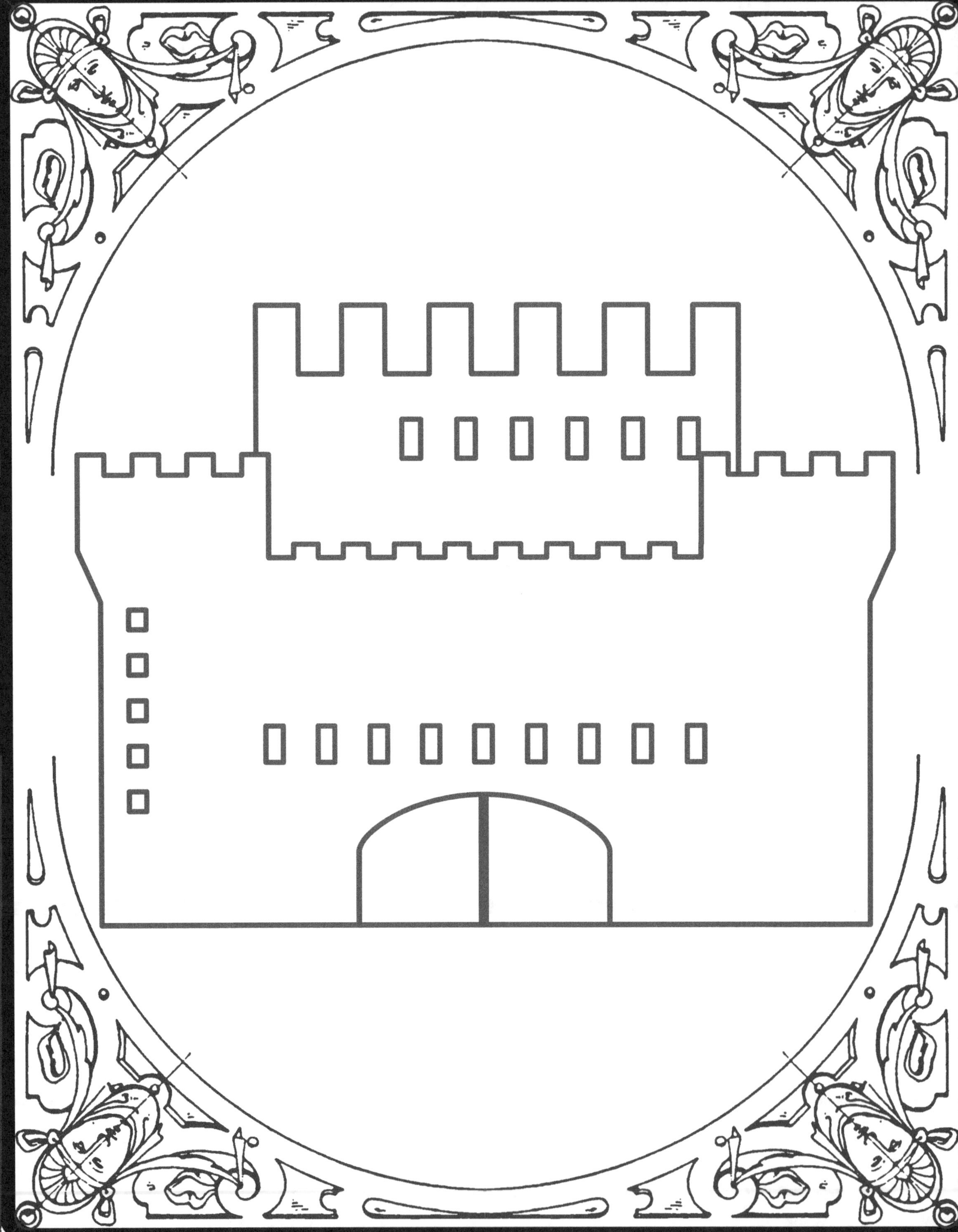

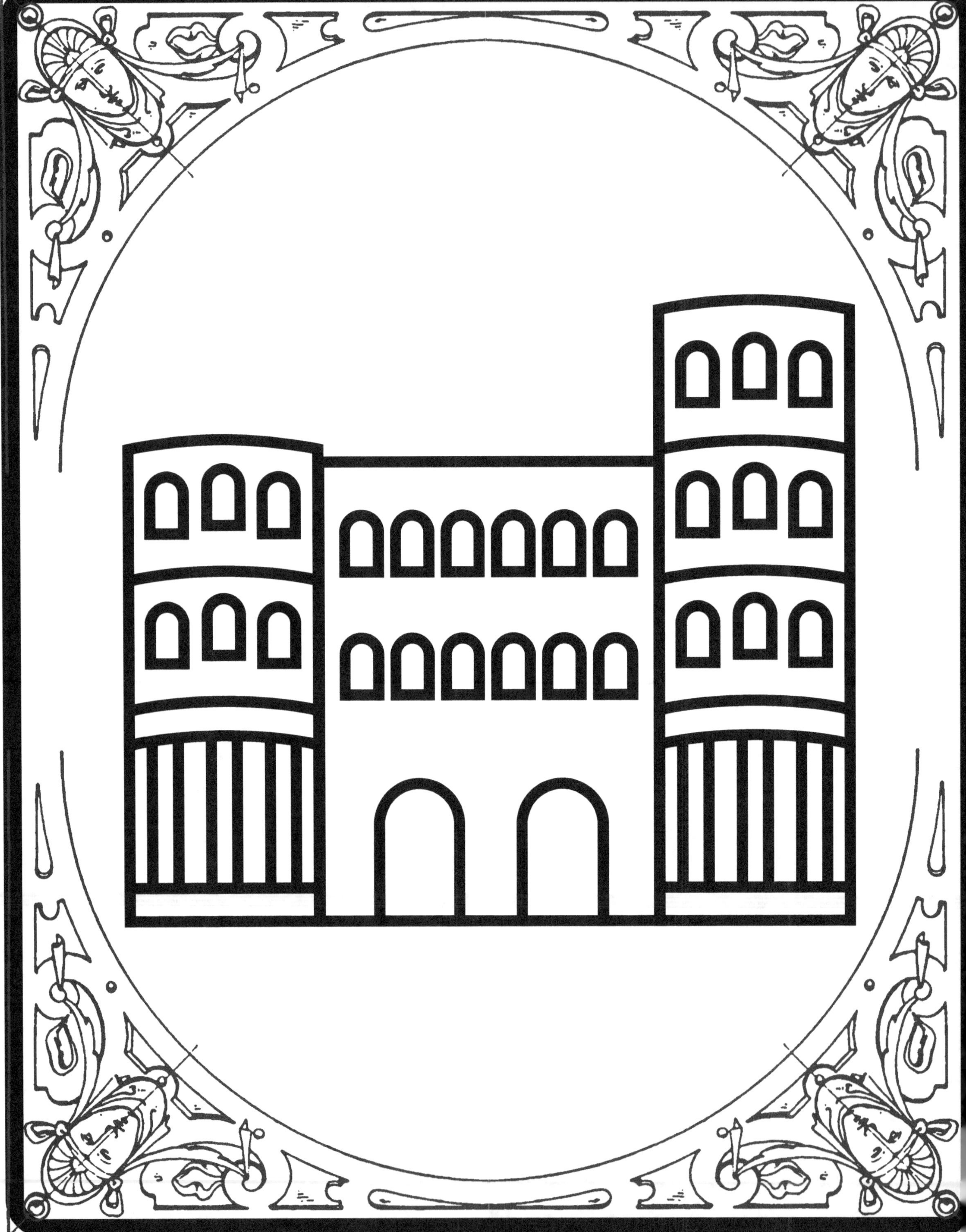

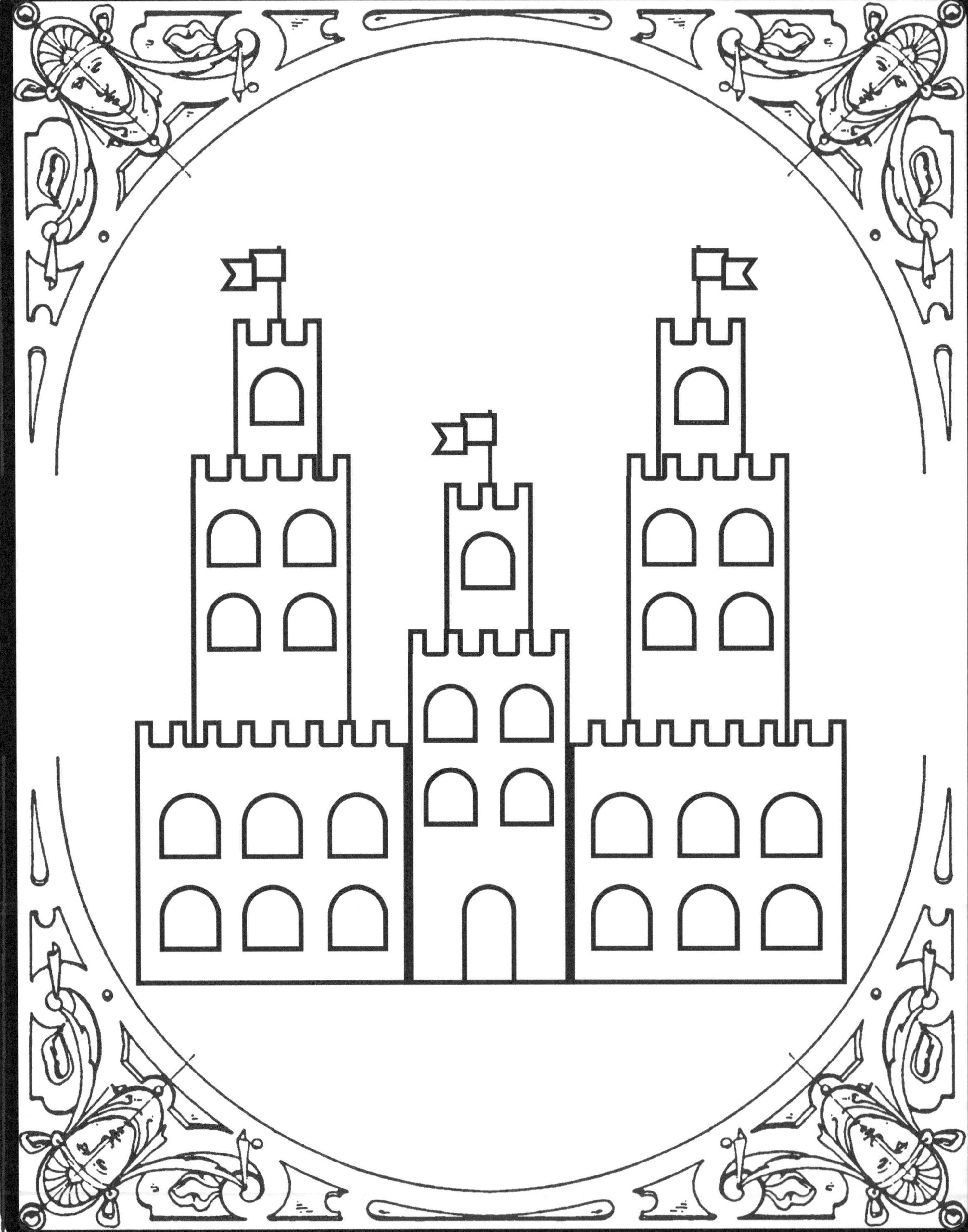

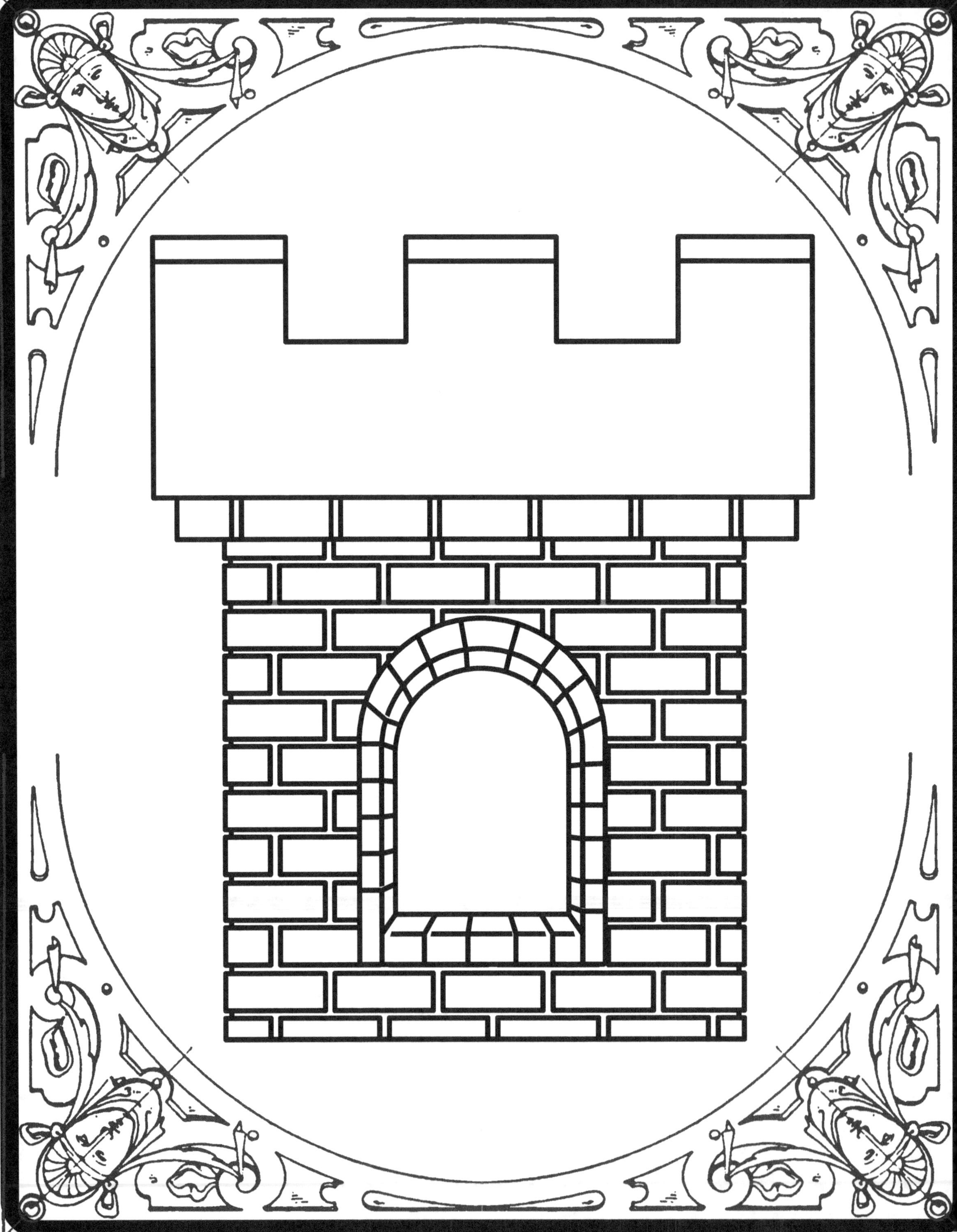

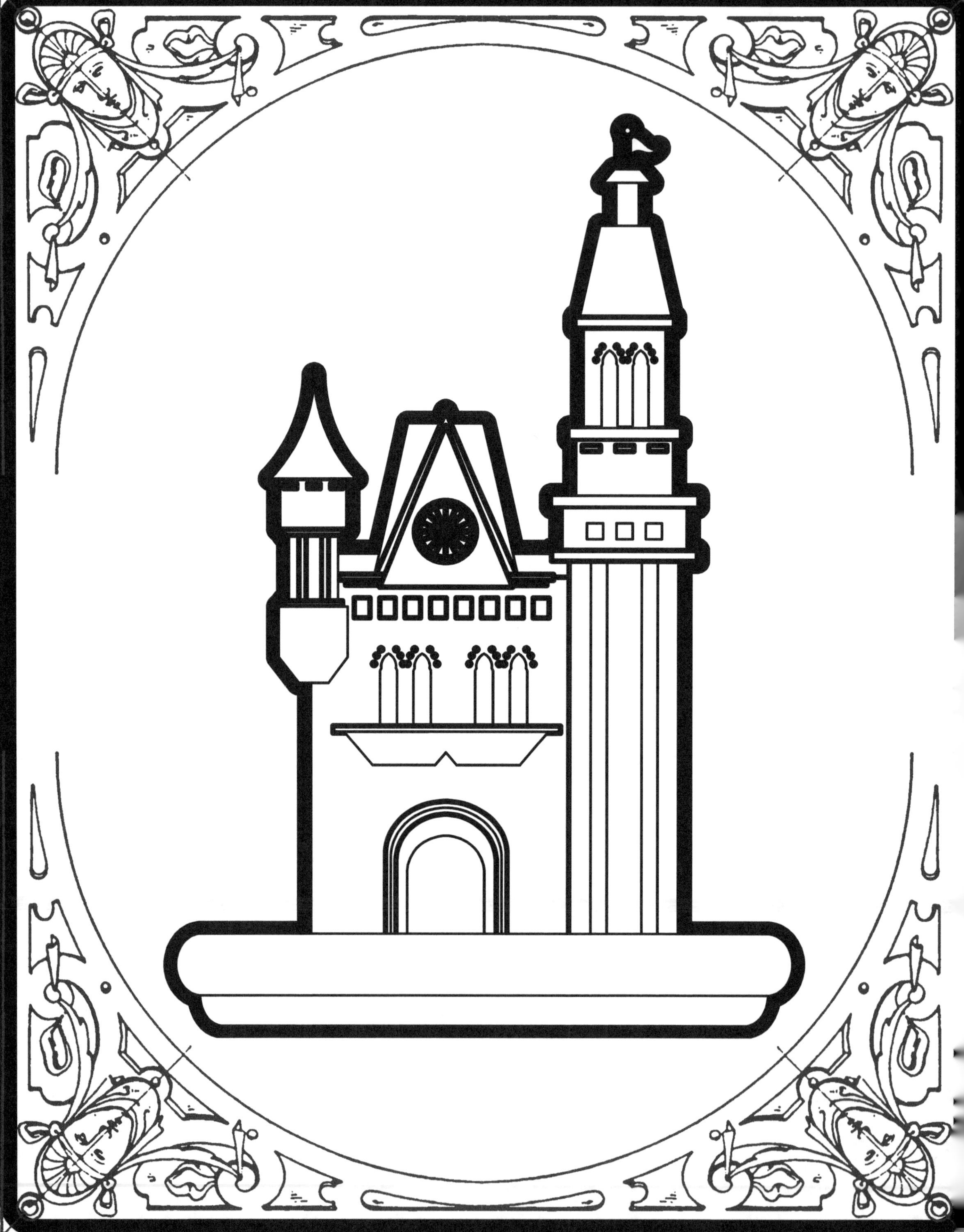

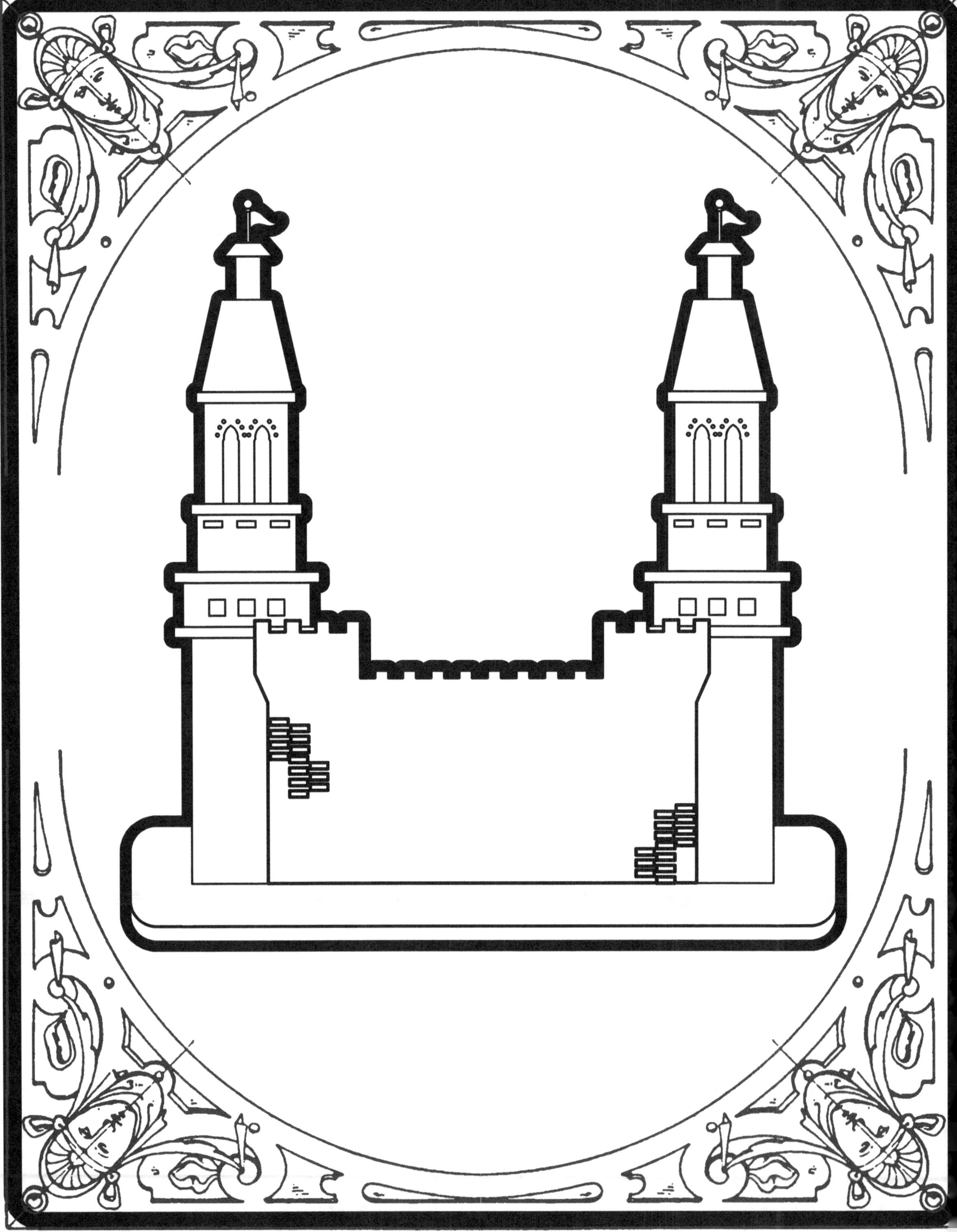

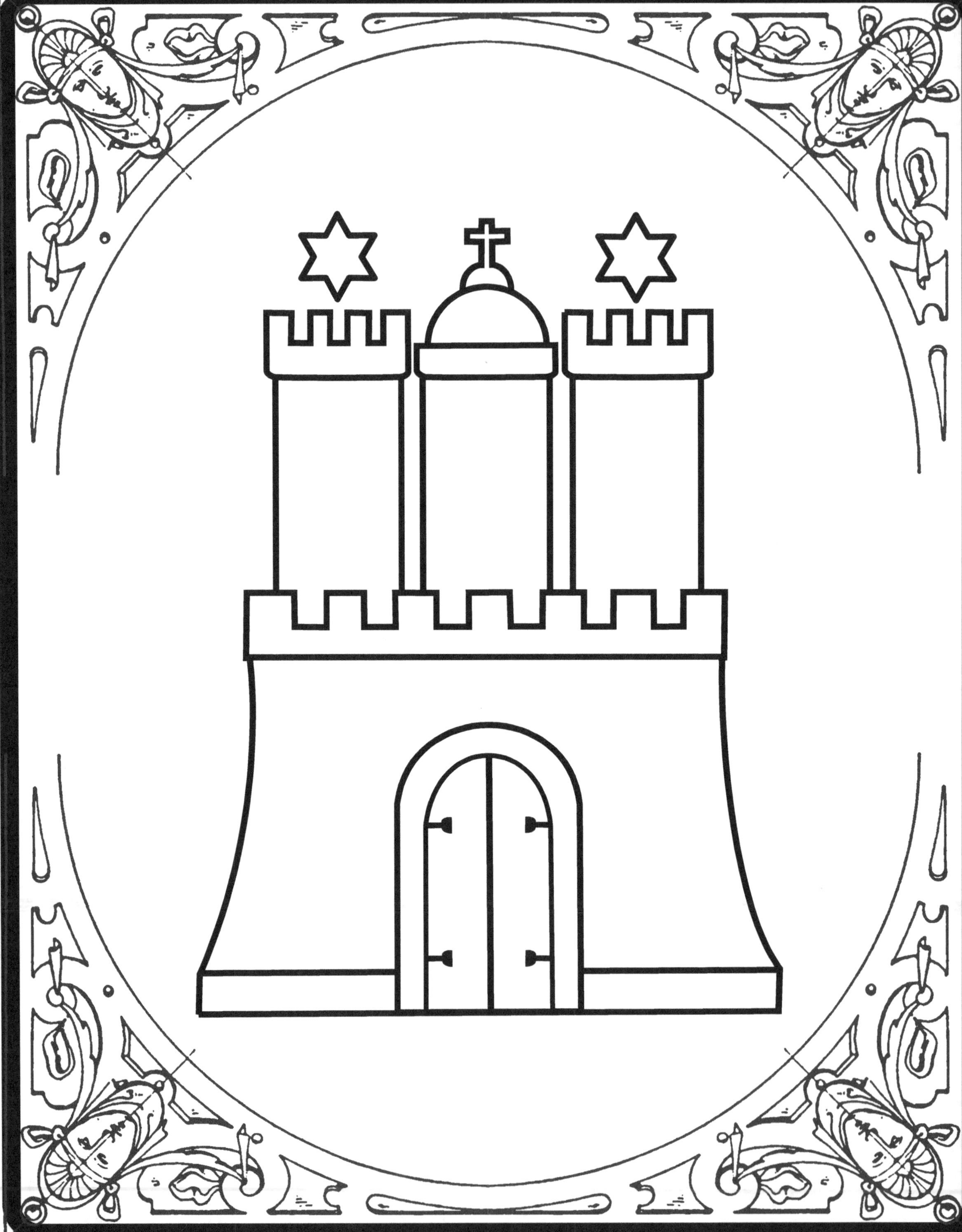

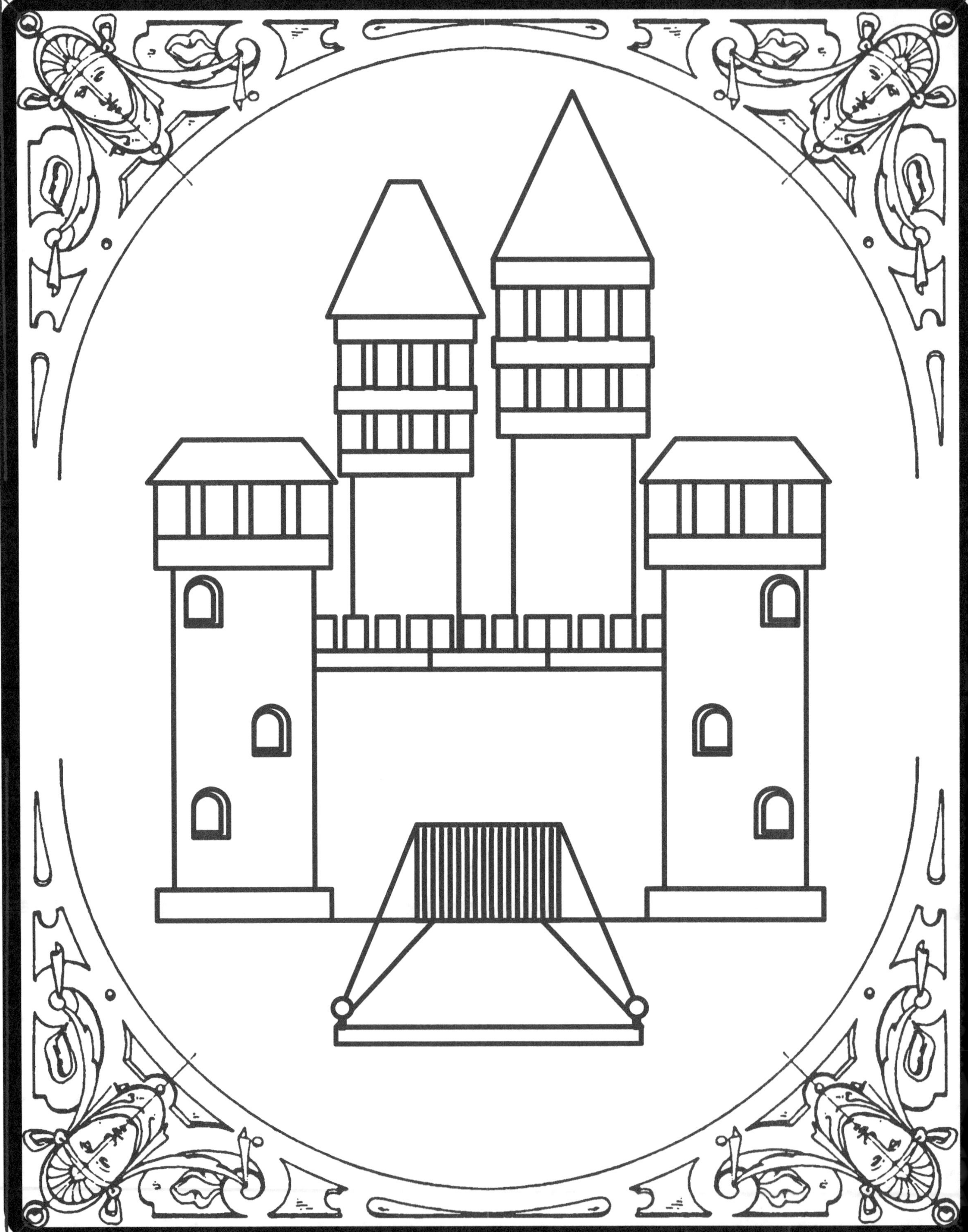

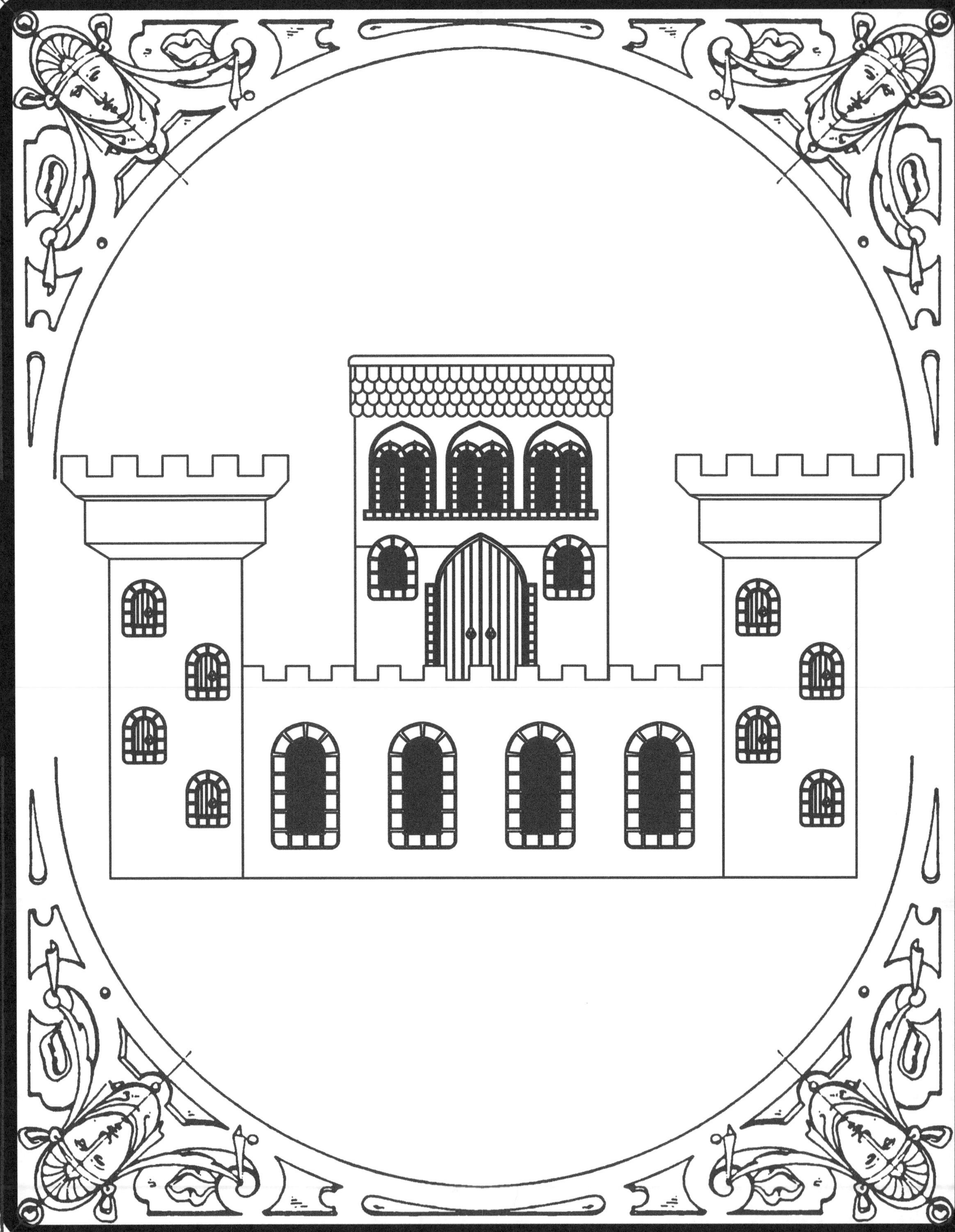

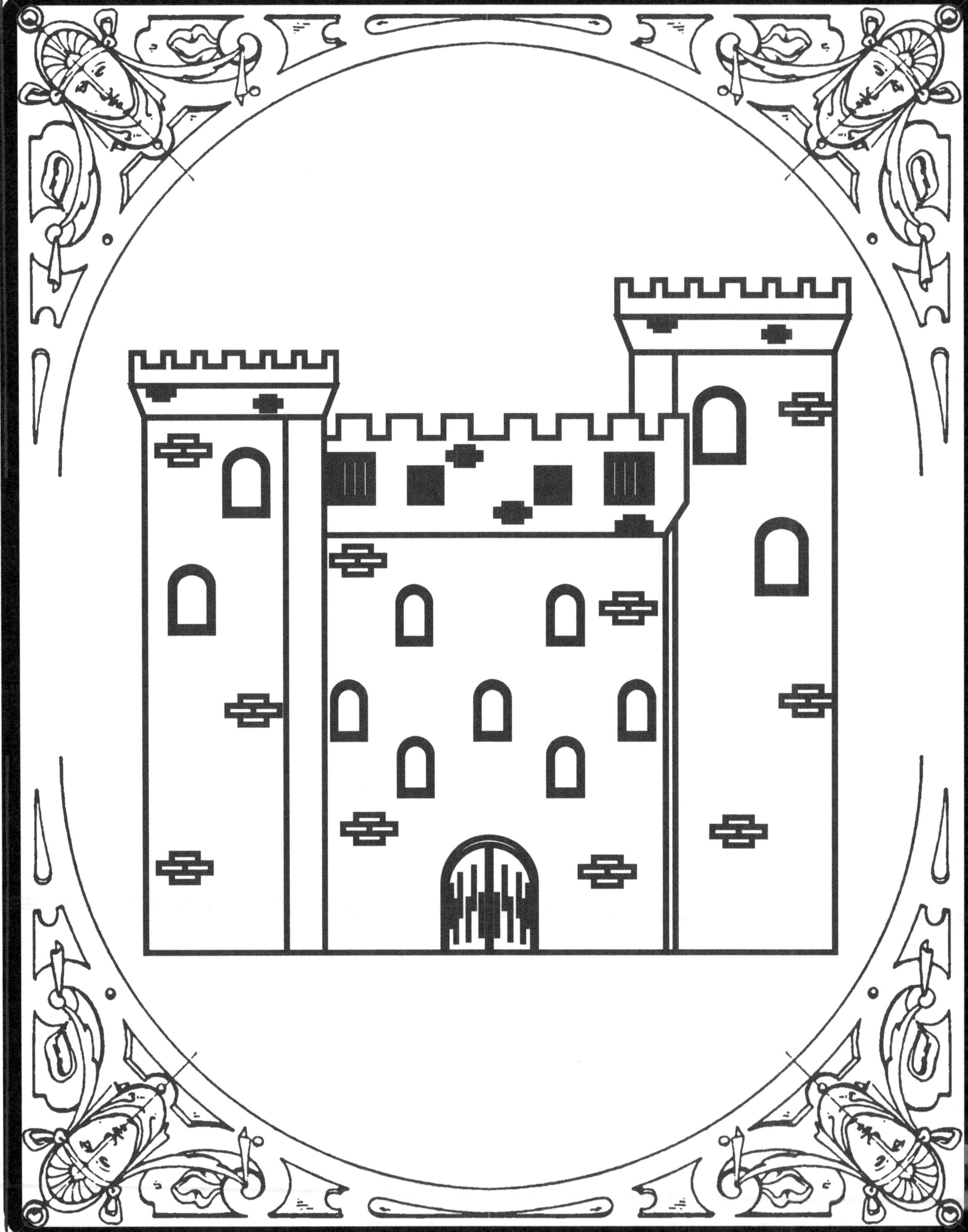

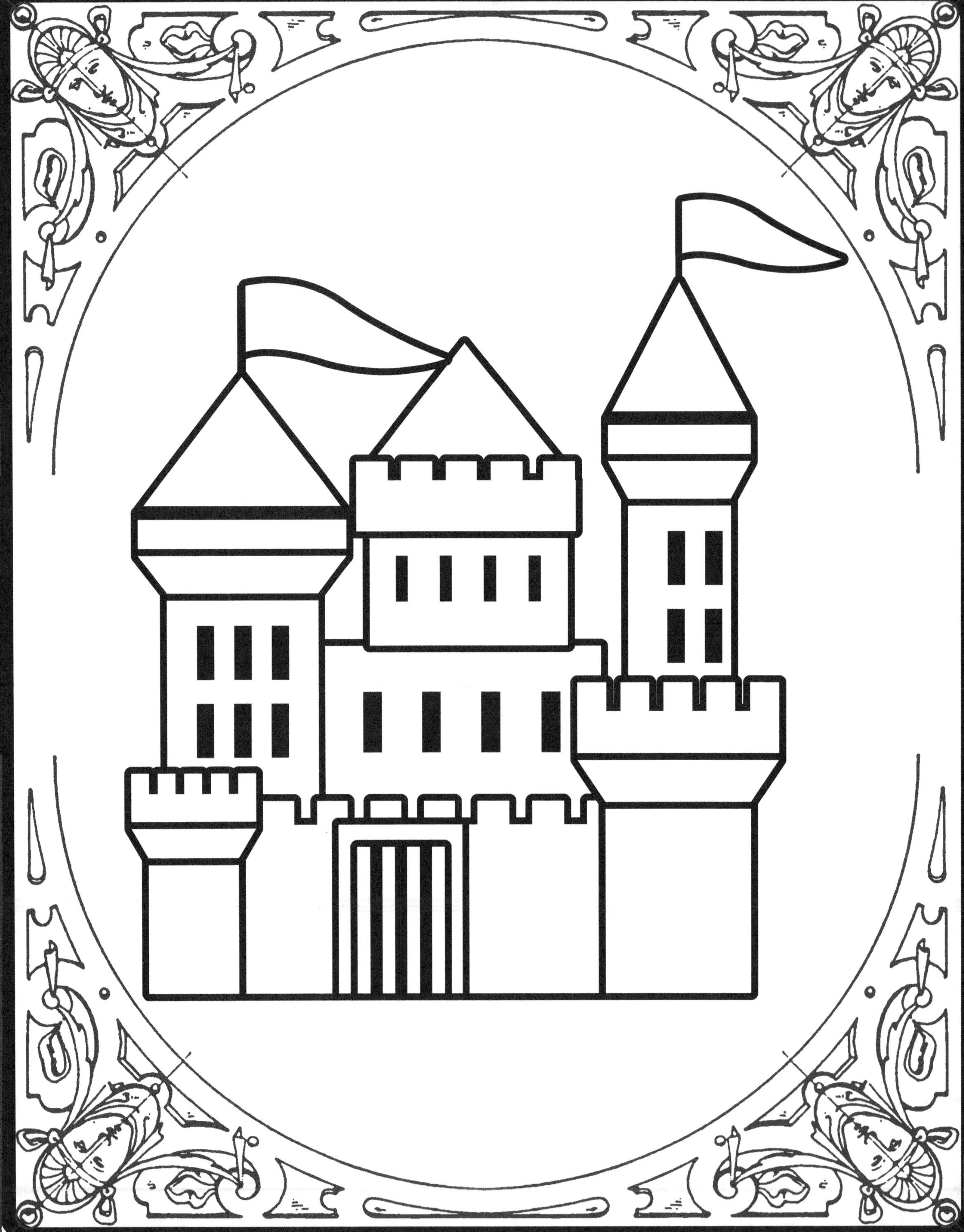

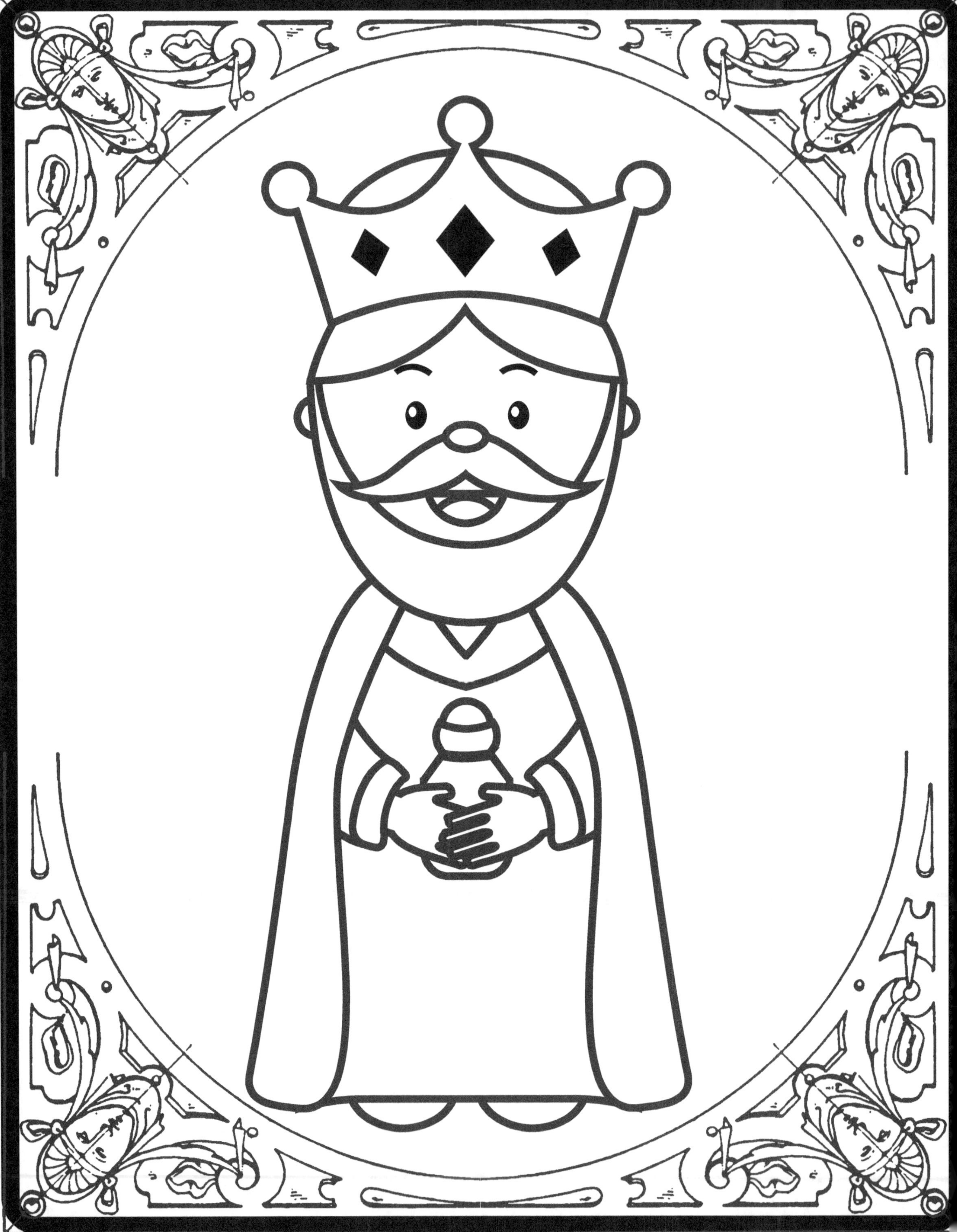

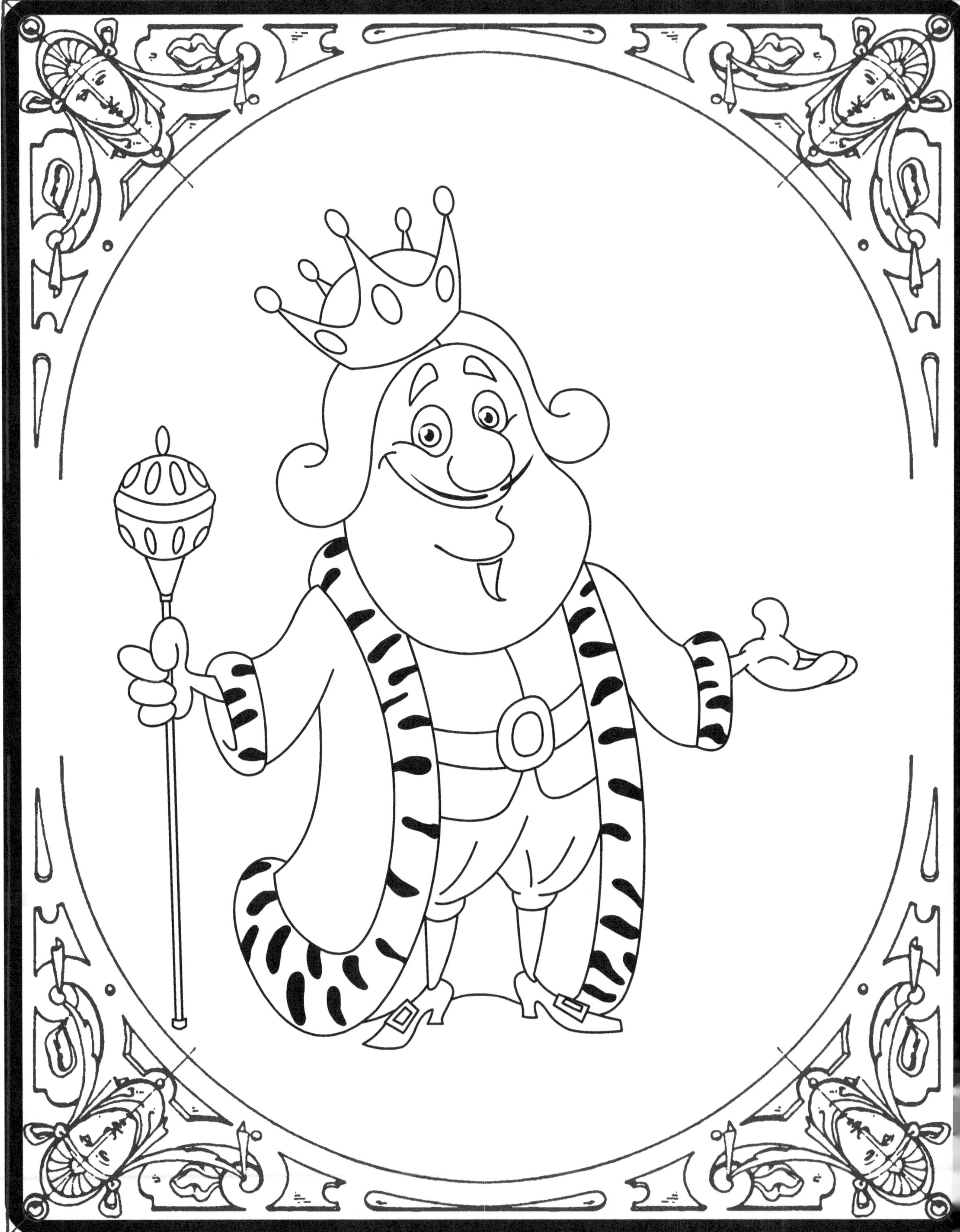

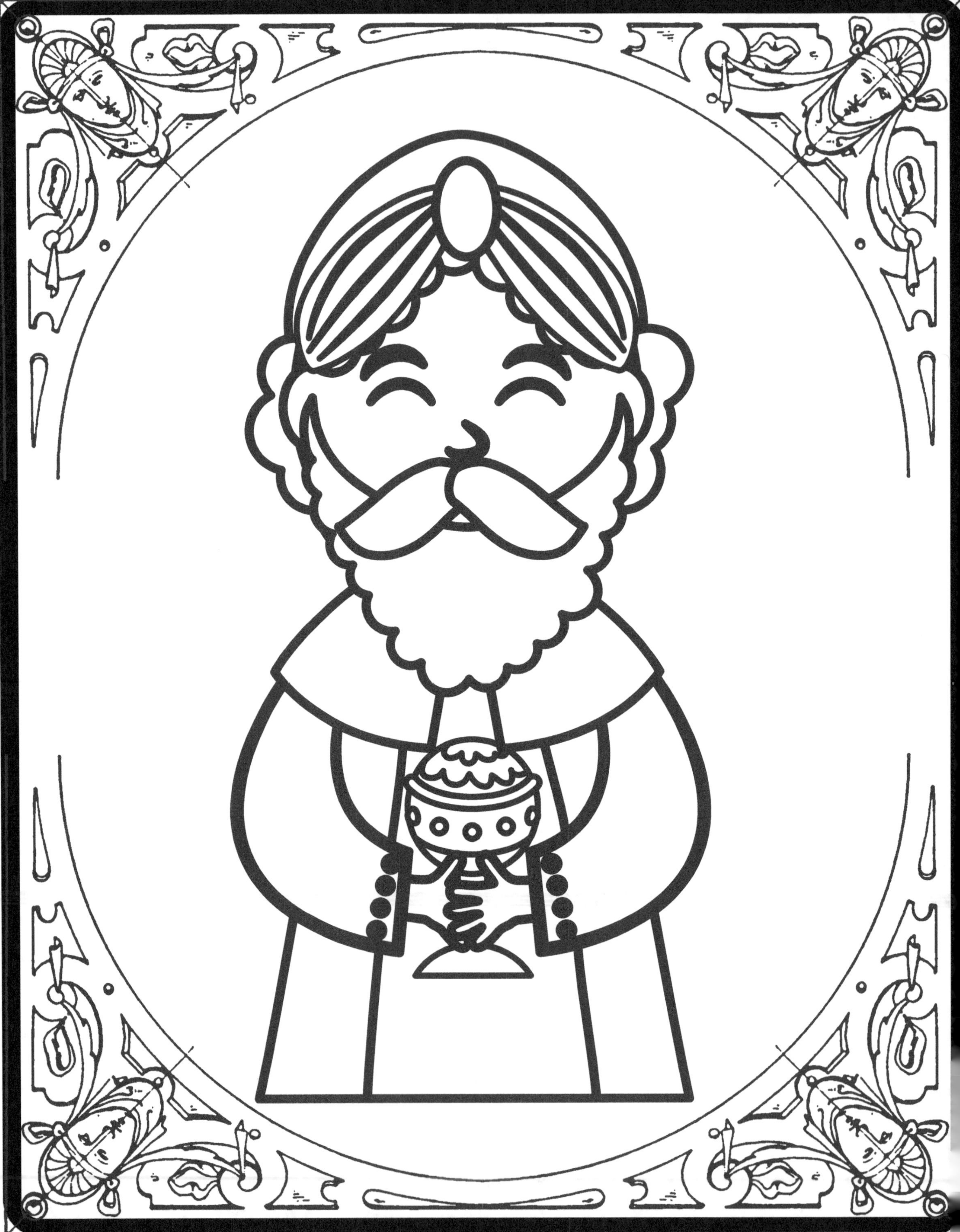

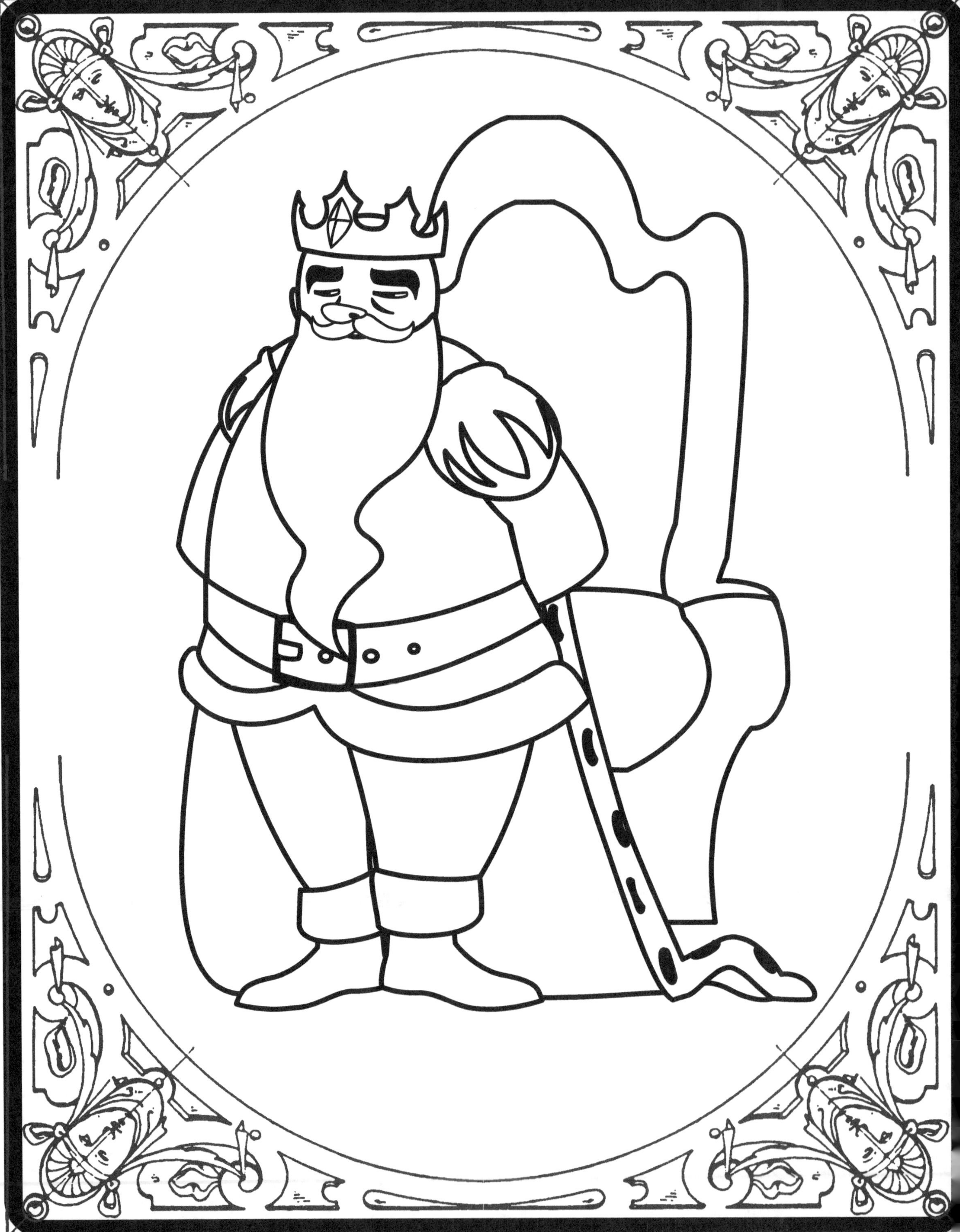

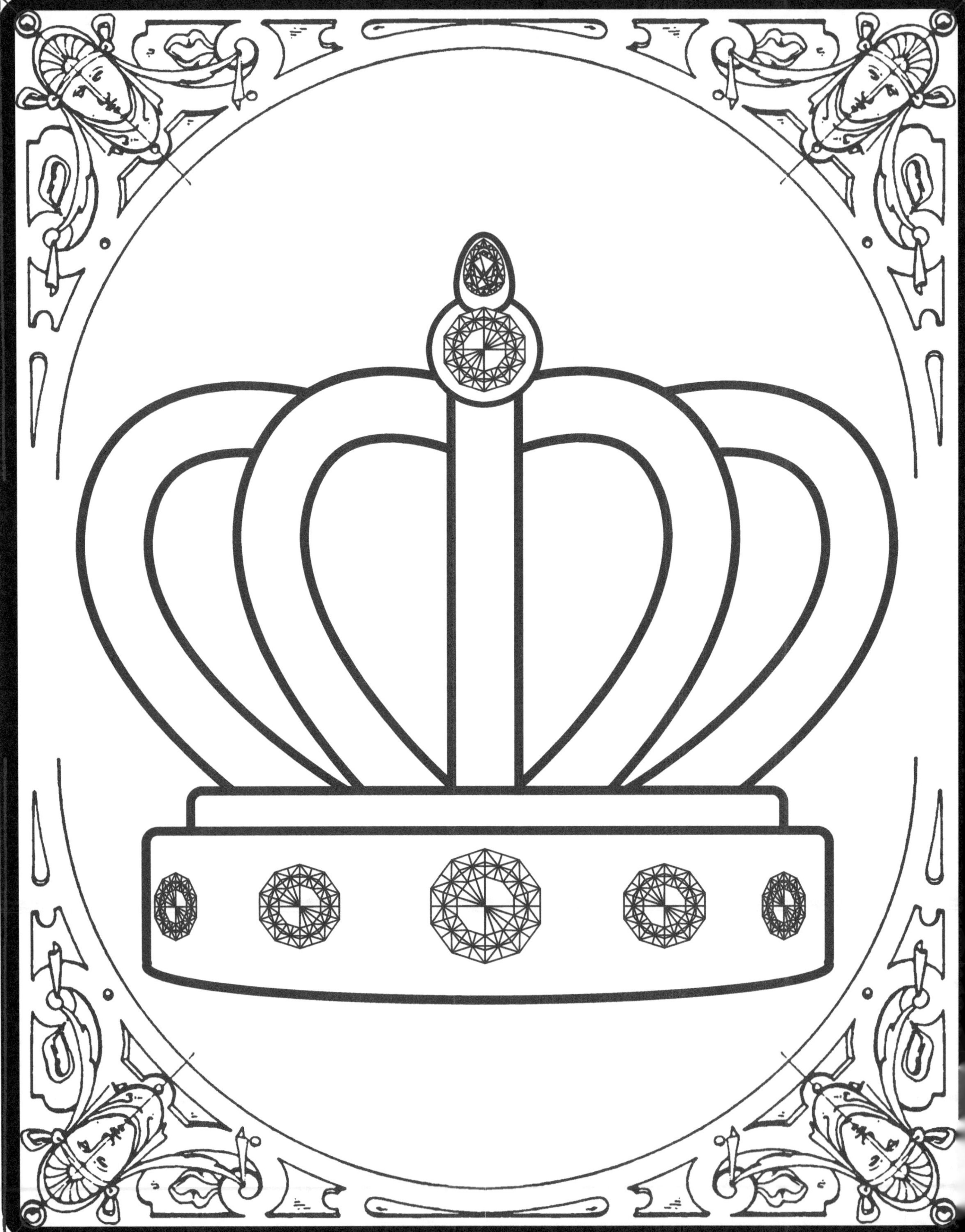

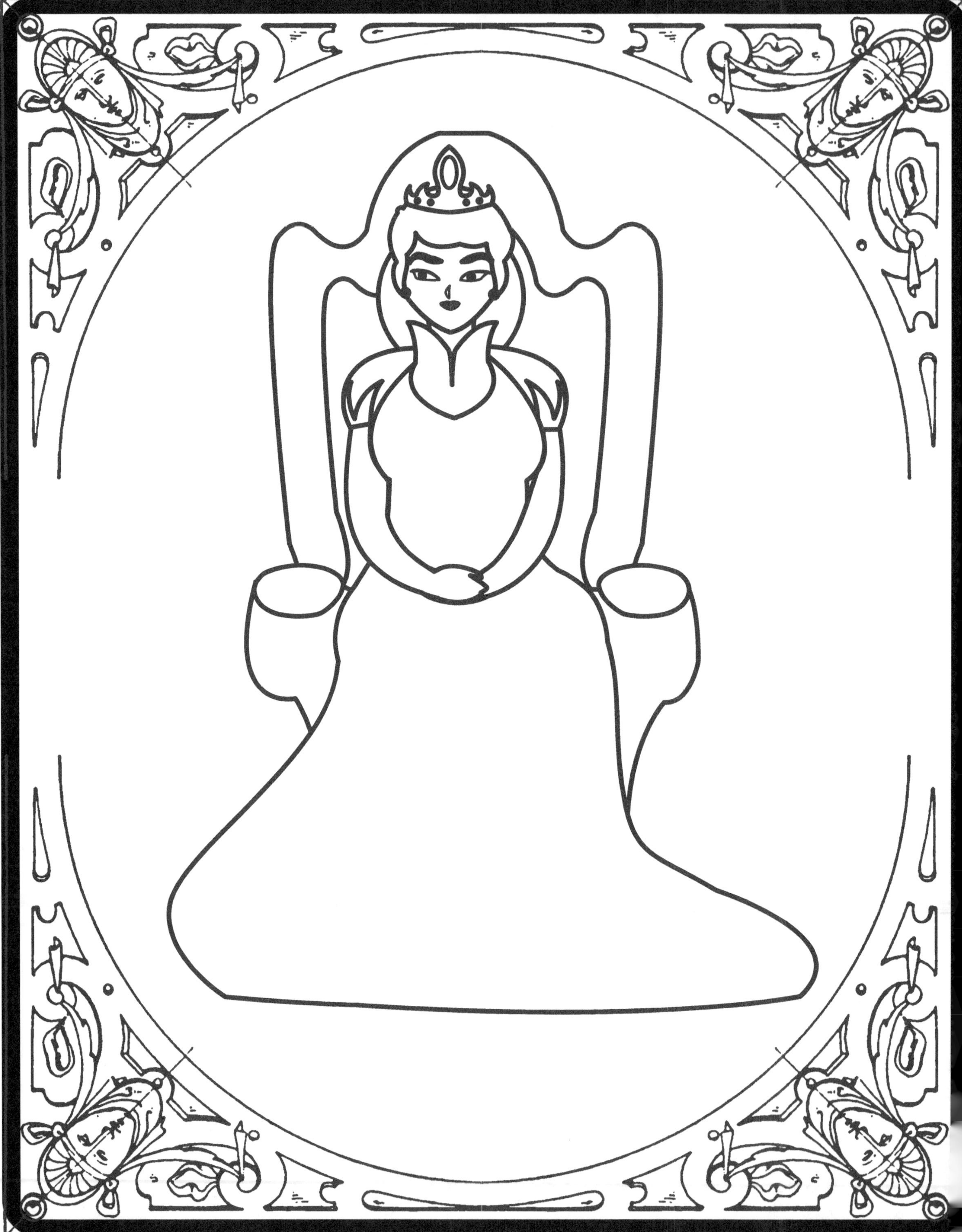

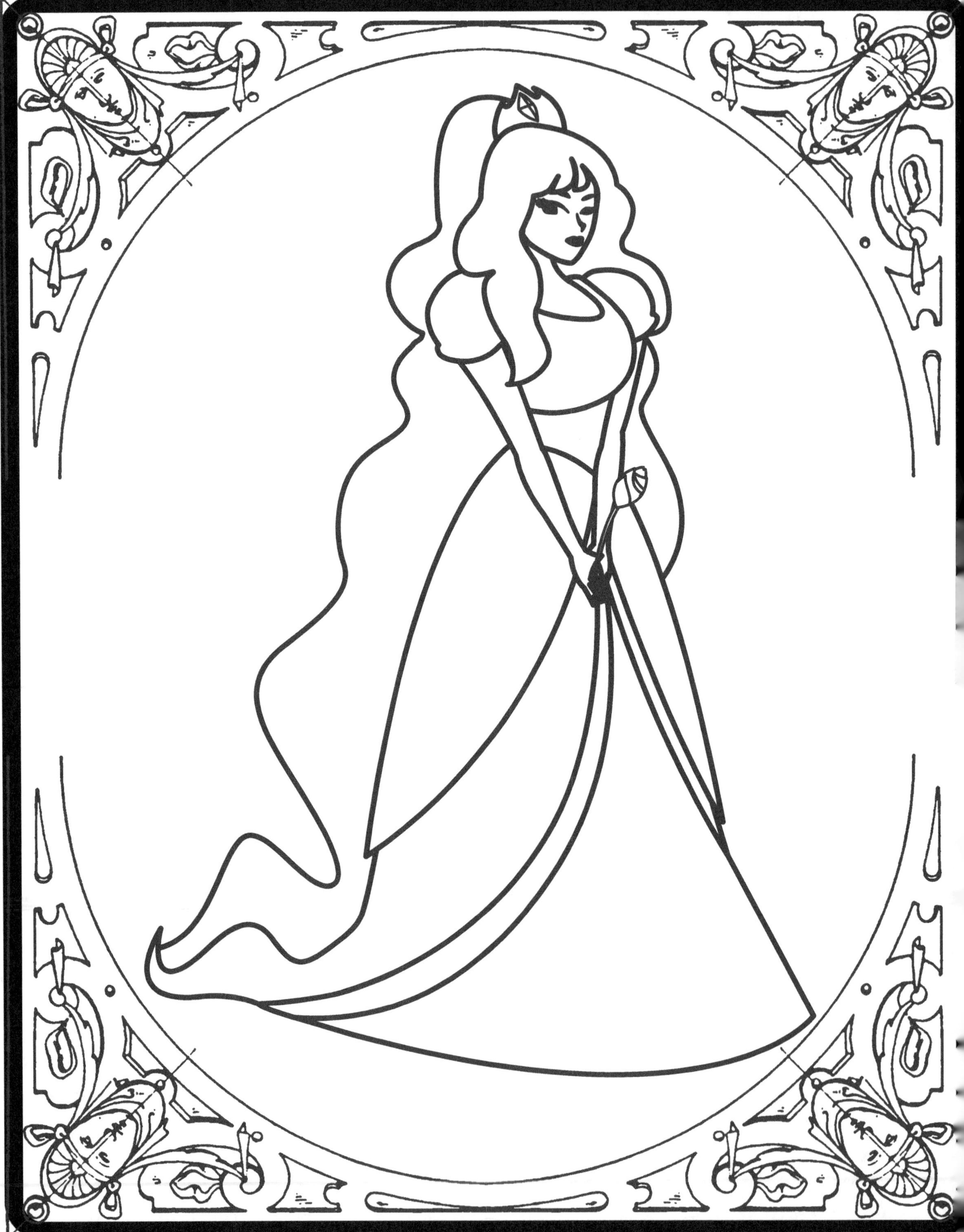

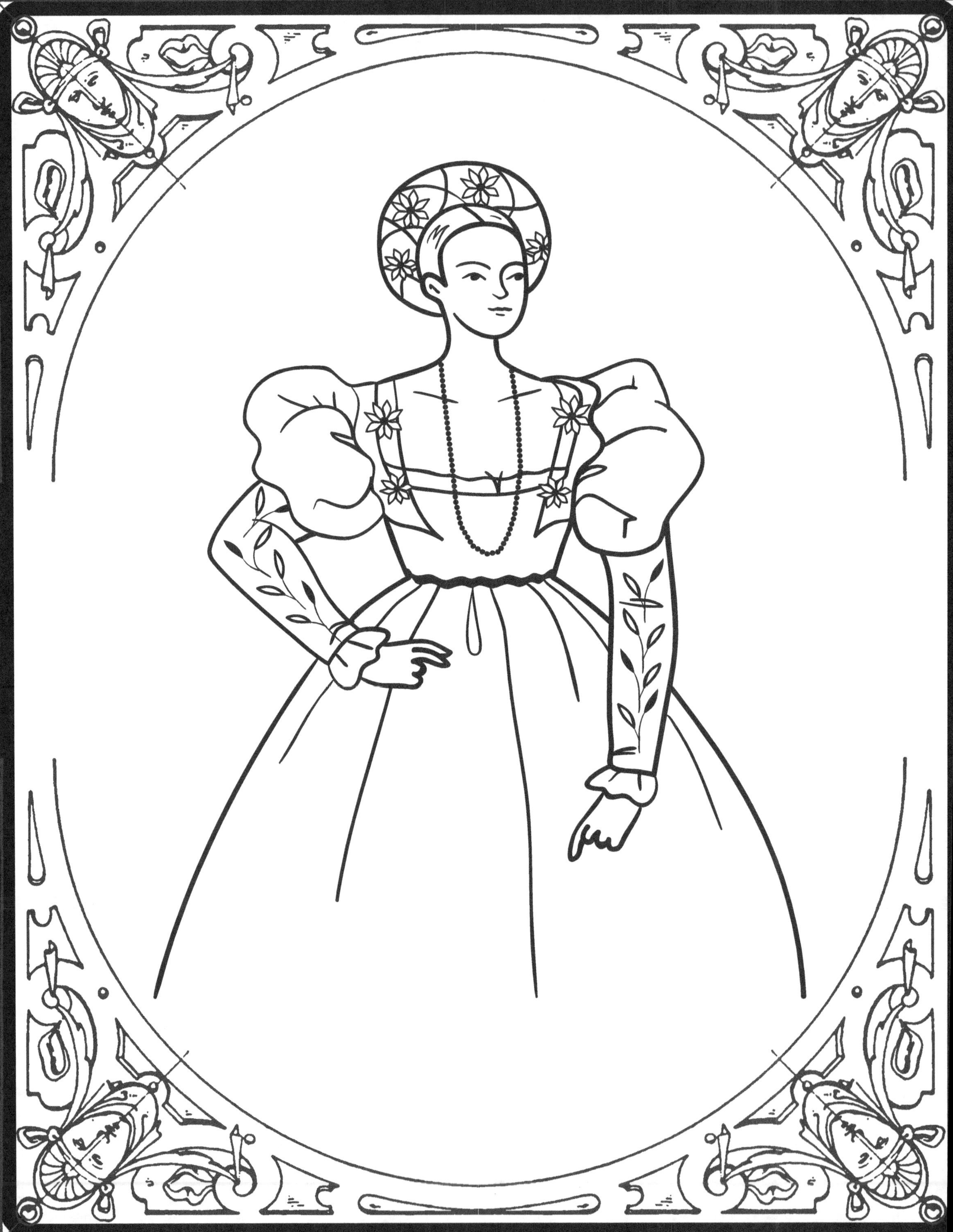

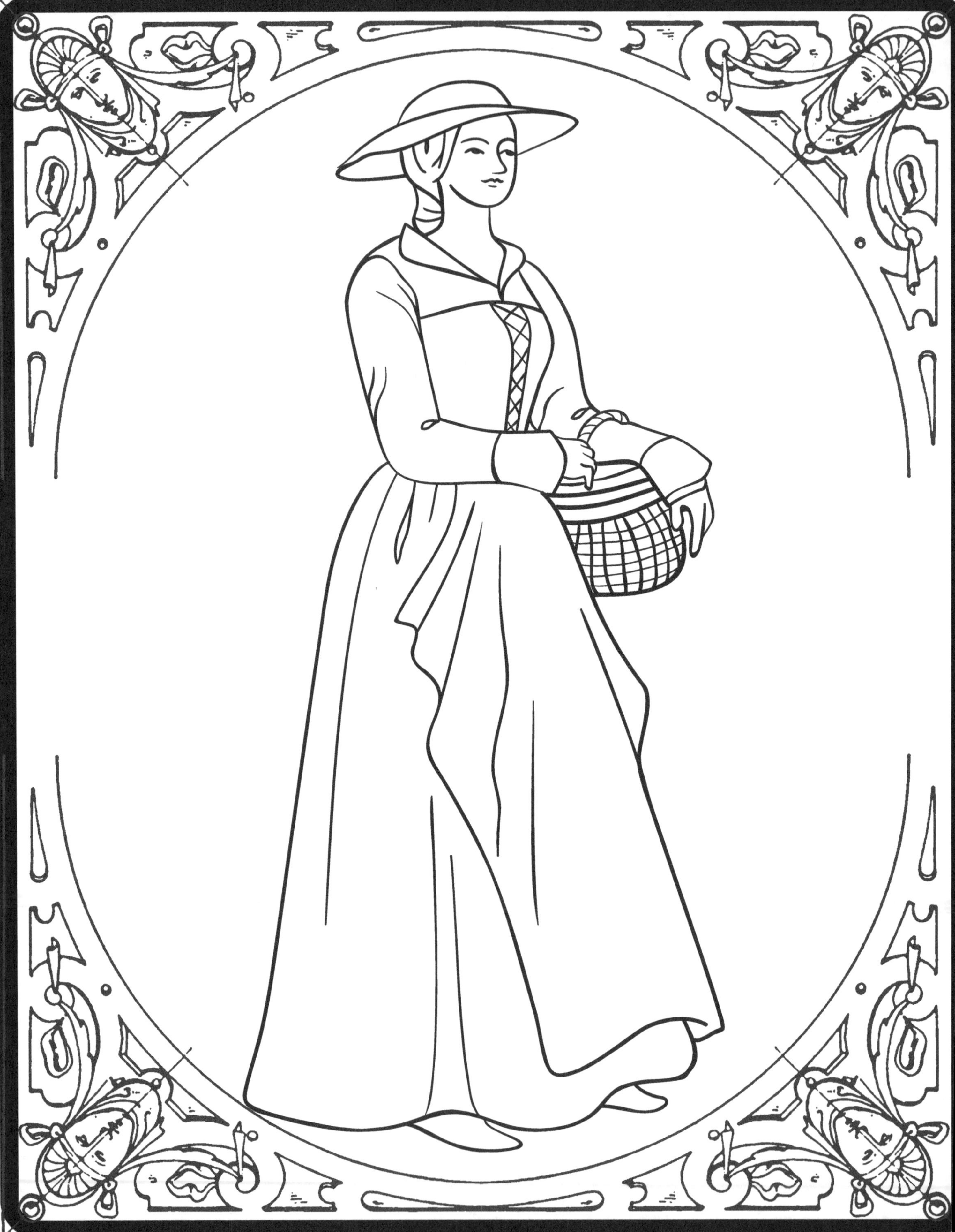

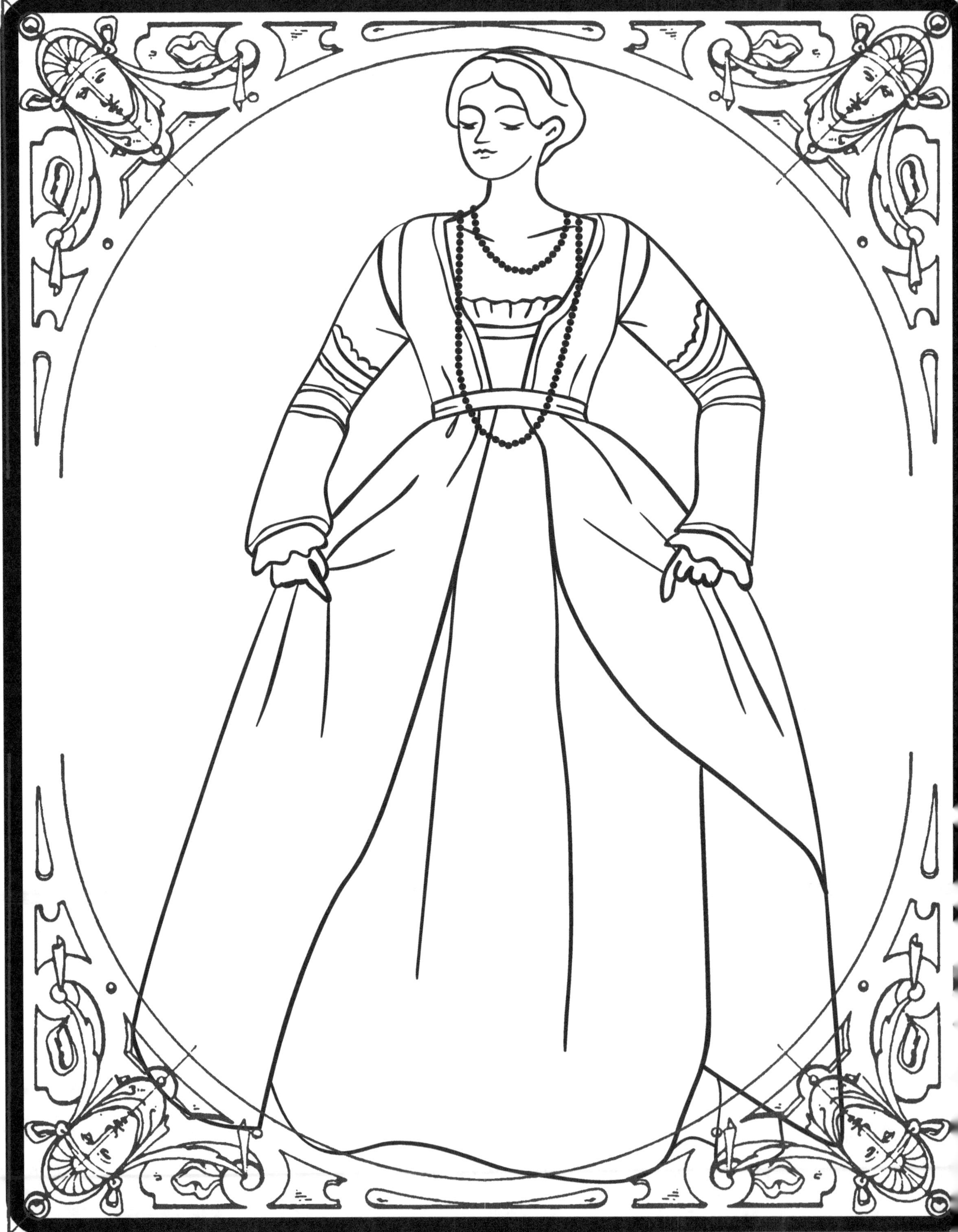

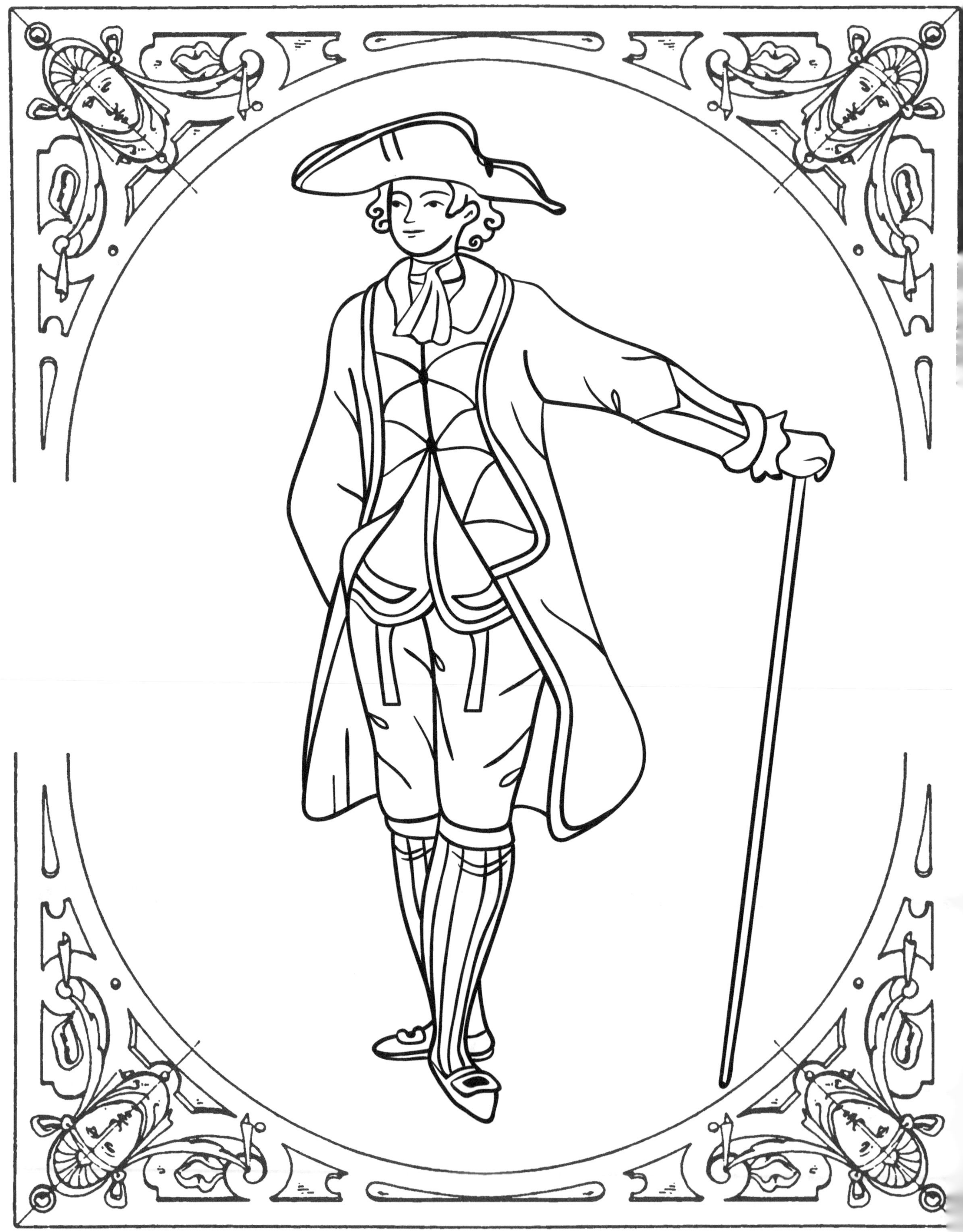

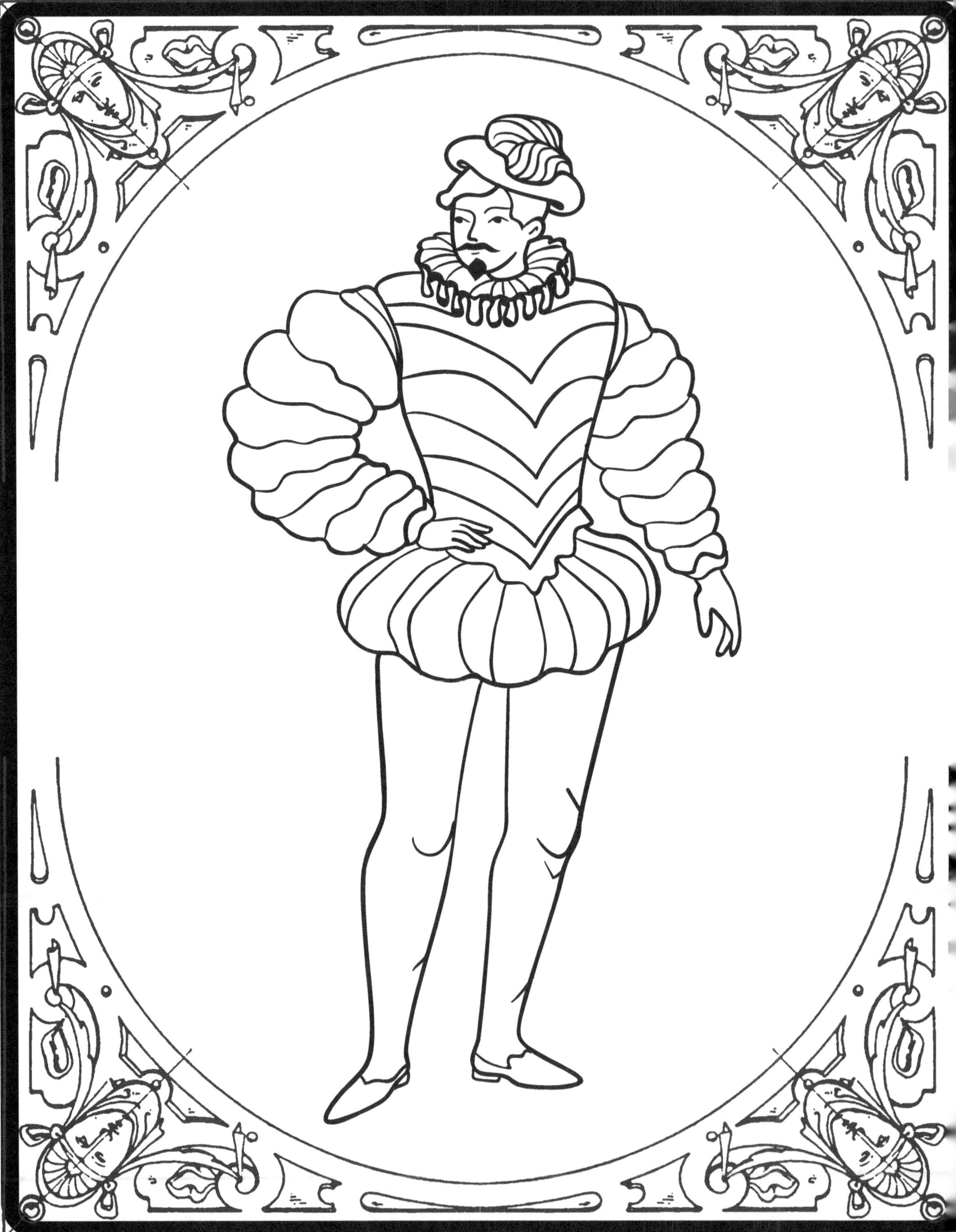

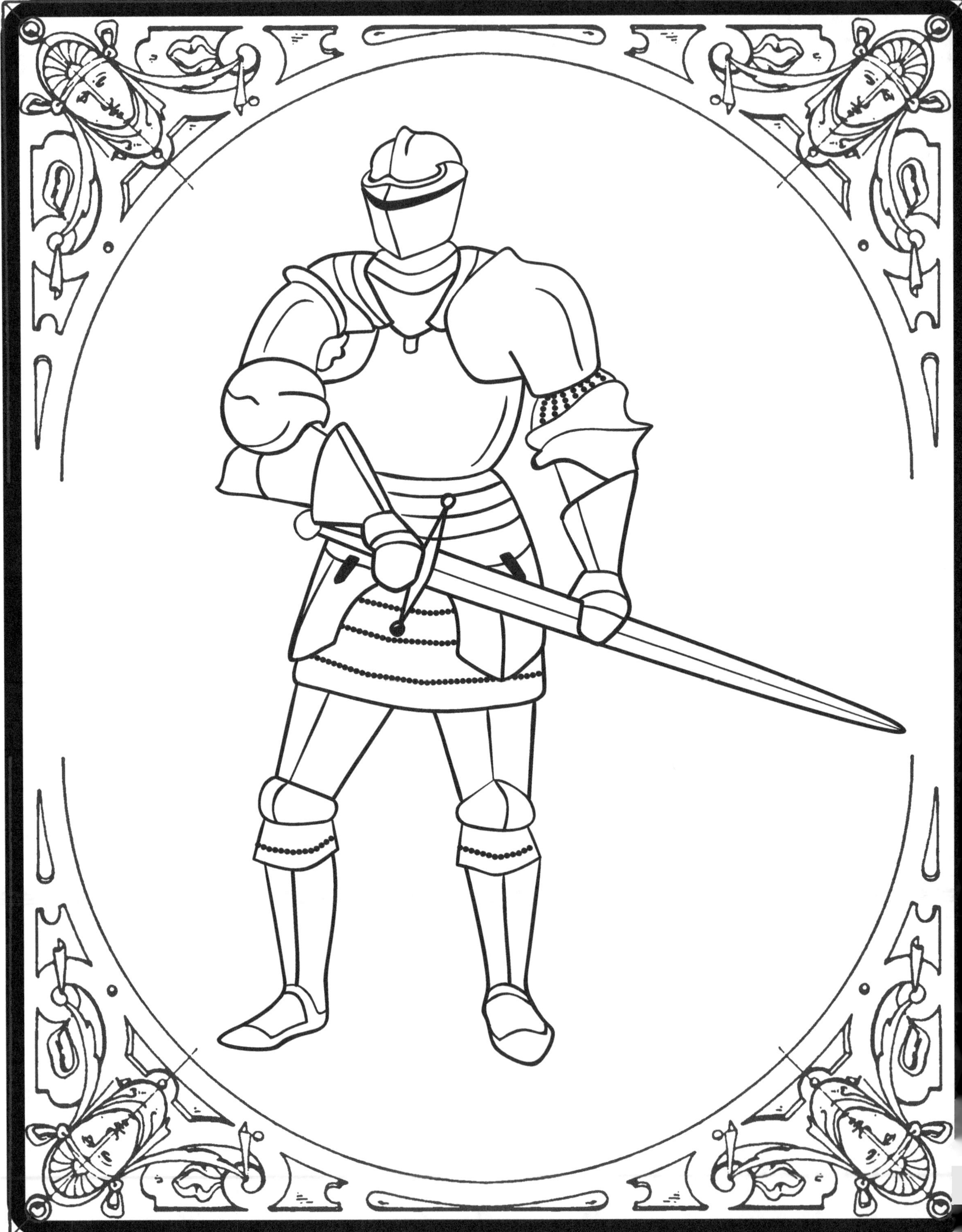

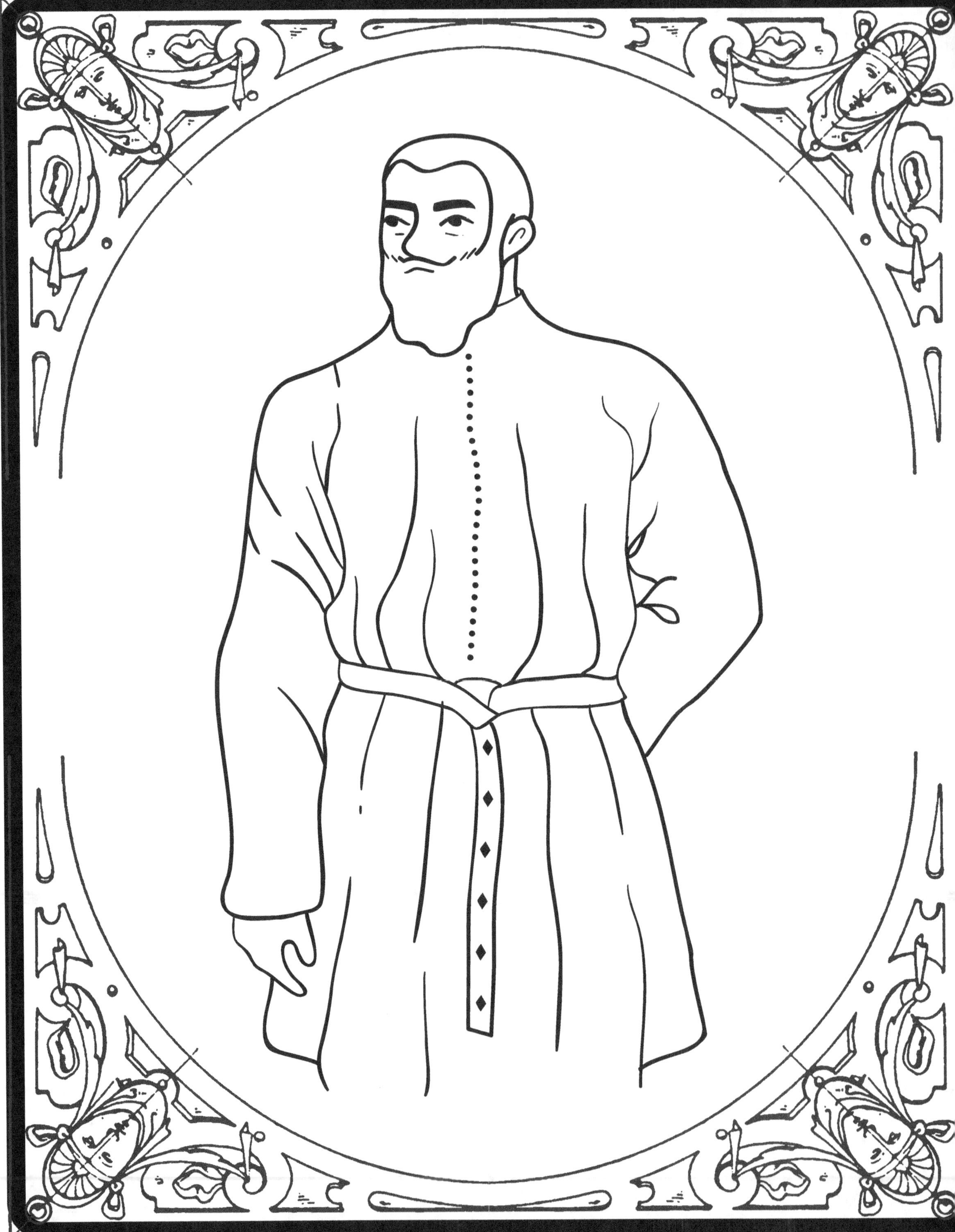

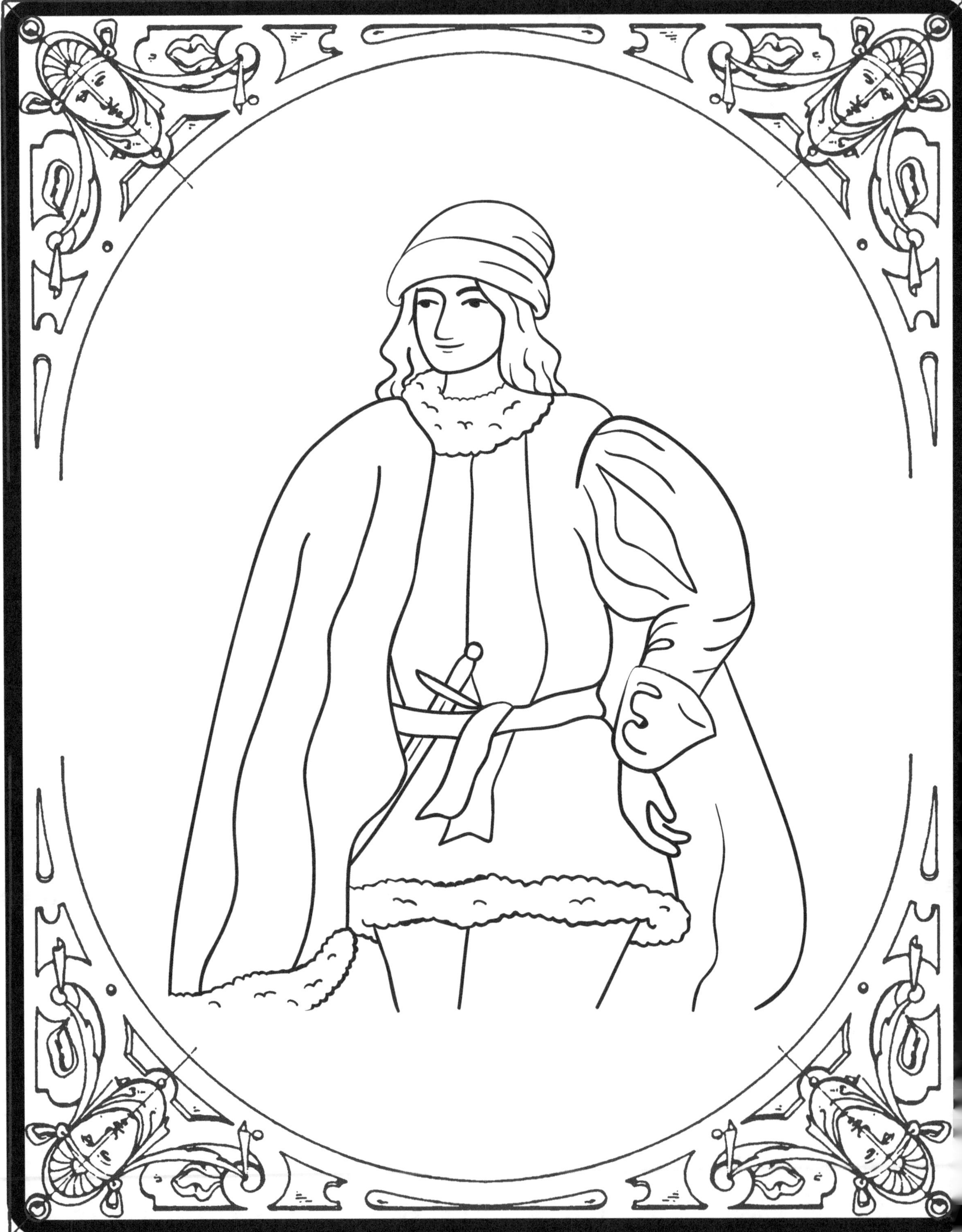

Thank you.

We hope to enjoyed our book.

As a small family company, your feedback is very impotant to us.

Please let us know how you like our book at

pvalverson@gmail.com